MY FAMILY MEDICAL HISTORY

Casey Murphy

This book came about after I was diagnosed with breast cancer.

Until then, my experience with the doctor's office was limited to one relatively easy childbirth.

Once diagnosed, the questions came flooding in. "How did your grandfather's uncle pass away" and "At what age did your great-aunt pass".

I had no idea. My family didn't exactly sit around the fireplace and talk about Uncle Gene's gout.

I was desperate for one place to put everything I had learned from asking the hard questions of family through the distraction of my diagnosis and it struck me that I did not want my daughter to have to deliver this kind of news and immediately follow up with invasive questions.

These things are important. The medical field is making strides in figuring out the answers to "why" and the doctors need your help to better heal you.

This book will help you answer these questions without worry; and what's more, it will help your children and grandchildren understand. Don't think of it as an invasion of privacy. Think of it as a helping hand to those you love.

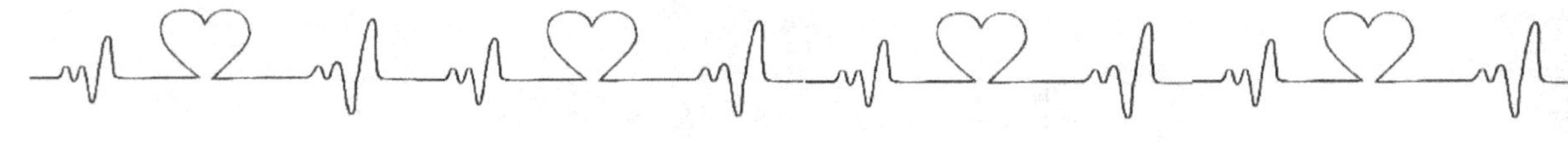

INSTRUCTIONS

Simple. Fill in the blanks.

Each page is for one member of your family. The first page should be yours, then your mother and Father.

Next should be your siblings. Include half-siblings, as they share part of your DNA. If you have half-aunts and uncles, add them as well

You can go back as far as you have information for.

Once you are finished with historical data, begin adding your children and your grandchildren.

I do not claim expertise in genetics, but I've done my fair share of research into the questions asked and the importance of giving as much information as possible.

There is a blank space at the end of each person's page. Use this space for any items of note that are not covered in the questionnaire.

NAME: ____

Date of Birth: _________ Date of Death: _________ State/country of birth: _________________

Part of a multiple birth? YES / NO

Spouse: _______________________________ Relation to main subject: _________________

Mother/Father of: _______________________________Child of: _______________________________

Ethnic Origin: ____

*For Ethnicity, please use "Irish, German, English", not "White" or use "Argentinian, Spanish, Brazilian", not "Hispanic". We will need to know where their roots are from.

Reason for Death: ____

Occupation/Trade: _______________________________ State/Country of death: _______________

~~~~~~

Was this person ever diagnosed with Cancer? _________

If so, at what age was the first diagnosis? _______

Type of Cancer:

BREAST   OVARIAN   COLON   PROSTATE   MELANOMA   _________________

LUNG   NON-HODGKIN LYMPHOMA   PANCREATIC   LEUKEMIA

What was the prognosis and treatment? Was treatment successful?

____

Was Genetic testing done and if so, were any mutations found that would indicate a higher chance of cancer? ____

Is there an occurrence of Ashkenazi Jewish ancestry? YES / NO

If yes, which family member does it originate from? _________________________
~~~~~~

Please check below if any of these conditions apply. For each check, please use the additional space for explanations. Things like age when diagnosed and severity are helpful.

- ♡ ARTHRITIS
- ♡ BIRTH DEFECTS
- ♡ HIGH CHOLESTROL
- ♡ MENTAL RETARDATION
- ♡ CLINICAL DEPRESSION
- ♡ MULTIPLE MISCARRIGAGES
- ♡ OBESITY
- ♡ OSTEOPOROSIS
- ♡ INFERTILITY
- ♡ EARLY/DELAYED PUBERTY
- ♡ SPECTRUM/AUTISM
- ♡ LUNG DISEASE
- ♡ KIDNEY DISEASE
- ♡ ALLERGIES TO MEDICATIONS

- ♡ HEARING LOSS
- ♡ HIGH BLOOD PRESSURE
- ♡ PHYSICAL ABNORMALITIES
- ♡ STROKE
- ♡ VISION LOSS
- ♡ ASTHMA
- ♡ DIABETES
- ♡ HEART DISEASE
- ♡ VERY TALL OR VERY SHORT STATURE
    *Compared to the rest of the family
- ♡ BIRTH MARKS
- ♡ BLOOD CLOTTING DISORDERS
- ♡ ALZHEIMER'S/DIMENTIA
- ♡ GOUT

NAME: ____

Date of Birth: _________ Date of Death: _________ State/country of birth: _________________

Part of a multiple birth? YES / NO

Spouse: _______________________________ Relation to main subject: _________________

Mother/Father of: _______________________________Child of: _________________________

Ethnic Origin: ____

*For Ethnicity, please use "Irish, German, English", not "White" or use "Argentinian, Spanish, Brazilian", not "Hispanic". We will need to know where their roots are from.

Reason for Death: ____

Occupation/Trade: _______________________________ State/Country of death: _______________

~~~~~~

Was this person ever diagnosed with Cancer? _________

If so, at what age was the first diagnosis? _______

Type of Cancer:

BREAST   OVARIAN   COLON   PROSTATE   MELANOMA   _________________

LUNG   NON-HODGKIN LYMPHOMA   PANCREATIC   LEUKEMIA

What was the prognosis and treatment? Was treatment successful?

____

Was Genetic testing done and if so, were any mutations found that would indicate a higher chance of cancer? ____

Is there an occurrence of Ashkenazi Jewish ancestry? YES / NO

If yes, which family member does it originate from? ___________________________
~~~~~~

Please check below if any of these conditions apply. For each check, please use the additional space for explanations. Things like age when diagnosed and severity are helpful.

- ♡ ARTHRITIS
- ♡ BIRTH DEFECTS
- ♡ HIGH CHOLESTROL
- ♡ MENTAL RETARDATION
- ♡ CLINICAL DEPRESSION
- ♡ MULTIPLE MISCARRIGAGES
- ♡ OBESITY
- ♡ OSTEOPOROSIS
- ♡ INFERTILITY
- ♡ EARLY/DELAYED PUBERTY
- ♡ SPECTRUM/AUTISM
- ♡ LUNG DISEASE
- ♡ KIDNEY DISEASE
- ♡ ALLERGIES TO MEDICATIONS

- ♡ HEARING LOSS
- ♡ HIGH BLOOD PRESSURE
- ♡ PHYSICAL ABNORMALITIES
- ♡ STROKE
- ♡ VISION LOSS
- ♡ ASTHMA
- ♡ DIABETES
- ♡ HEART DISEASE
- ♡ VERY TALL OR VERY SHORT STATURE
    *Compared to the rest of the family
- ♡ BIRTH MARKS
- ♡ BLOOD CLOTTING DISORDERS
- ♡ ALZHEIMER'S/DIMENTIA
- ♡ GOUT

NAME: ____

Date of Birth: __________ Date of Death: __________ State/country of birth: ___________________

Part of a multiple birth? YES / NO

Spouse: _______________________________ Relation to main subject: ____________________

Mother/Father of: _______________________________Child of: ___________________________

Ethnic Origin: ____

*For Ethnicity, please use "Irish, German, English", not "White" or use "Argentinian, Spanish, Brazilian", not "Hispanic". We will need to know where their roots are from.

Reason for Death: ____

Occupation/Trade: _______________________________ State/Country of death: ______________

~~~~~~

Was this person ever diagnosed with Cancer? __________

If so, at what age was the first diagnosis? _______

Type of Cancer:

BREAST   OVARIAN   COLON   PROSTATE   MELANOMA   ________________

LUNG   NON-HODGKIN LYMPHOMA   PANCREATIC   LEUKEMIA

What was the prognosis and treatment? Was treatment successful?

____

Was Genetic testing done and if so, were any mutations found that would indicate a higher chance of cancer? ____

Is there an occurrence of Ashkenazi Jewish ancestry? YES / NO

If yes, which family member does it originate from? ____________________________
~~~~~~

Please check below if any of these conditions apply. For each check, please use the additional space for explanations. Things like age when diagnosed and severity are helpful.

♡ ARTHRITIS
♡ BIRTH DEFECTS
♡ HIGH CHOLESTROL
♡ MENTAL RETARDATION
♡ CLINICAL DEPRESSION
♡ MULTIPLE MISCARRIGAGES
♡ OBESITY
♡ OSTEOPOROSIS
♡ INFERTILITY
♡ EARLY/DELAYED PUBERTY
♡ SPECTRUM/AUTISM
♡ LUNG DISEASE
♡ KIDNEY DISEASE
♡ ALLERGIES TO MEDICATIONS

♡ HEARING LOSS
♡ HIGH BLOOD PRESSURE
♡ PHYSICAL ABNORMALITIES
♡ STROKE
♡ VISION LOSS
♡ ASTHMA
♡ DIABETES
♡ HEART DISEASE
♡ VERY TALL OR VERY SHORT STATURE
     *Compared to the rest of the family
♡ BIRTH MARKS
♡ BLOOD CLOTTING DISORDERS
♡ ALZHEIMER'S/DIMENTIA
♡ GOUT

NAME: ____

Date of Birth: __________   Date of Death: __________   State/country of birth: ____________________

Part of a multiple birth? YES / NO

Spouse: ______________________________   Relation to main subject: __________________

Mother/Father of: ______________________________Child of: ______________________________

Ethnic Origin: ____

*For Ethnicity, please use "Irish, German, English", not "White" or use "Argentinian, Spanish, Brazilian", not "Hispanic". We will need to know where their roots are from.

Reason for Death: ____

Occupation/Trade: ______________________________   State/Country of death: ________________

~~~~~~

Was this person ever diagnosed with Cancer? __________

If so, at what age was the first diagnosis? ______

Type of Cancer:

BREAST   OVARIAN   COLON   PROSTATE   MELANOMA   ____________________

LUNG   NON-HODGKIN LYMPHOMA   PANCREATIC   LEUKEMIA

What was the prognosis and treatment? Was treatment successful?

____

Was Genetic testing done and if so, were any mutations found that would indicate a higher chance of cancer? ____

Is there an occurrence of Ashkenazi Jewish ancestry? YES / NO

If yes, which family member does it originate from? ____________________
~~~~~~

Please check below if any of these conditions apply. For each check, please use the additional space for explanations. Things like age when diagnosed and severity are helpful.

- ♡ ARTHRITIS
- ♡ BIRTH DEFECTS
- ♡ HIGH CHOLESTROL
- ♡ MENTAL RETARDATION
- ♡ CLINICAL DEPRESSION
- ♡ MULTIPLE MISCARRIGAGES
- ♡ OBESITY
- ♡ OSTEOPOROSIS
- ♡ INFERTILITY
- ♡ EARLY/DELAYED PUBERTY
- ♡ SPECTRUM/AUTISM
- ♡ LUNG DISEASE
- ♡ KIDNEY DISEASE
- ♡ ALLERGIES TO MEDICATIONS

- ♡ HEARING LOSS
- ♡ HIGH BLOOD PRESSURE
- ♡ PHYSICAL ABNORMALITIES
- ♡ STROKE
- ♡ VISION LOSS
- ♡ ASTHMA
- ♡ DIABETES
- ♡ HEART DISEASE
- ♡ VERY TALL OR VERY SHORT STATURE
    *Compared to the rest of the family
- ♡ BIRTH MARKS
- ♡ BLOOD CLOTTING DISORDERS
- ♡ ALZHEIMER'S/DIMENTIA
- ♡ GOUT

NAME: ____

Date of Birth: _________ Date of Death: _________ State/country of birth: _________________

Part of a multiple birth? YES / NO

Spouse: _______________________________ Relation to main subject: __________________

Mother/Father of: _______________________________Child of: _______________________________

Ethnic Origin: ____

*For Ethnicity, please use "Irish, German, English", not "White" or use "Argentinian, Spanish, Brazilian", not "Hispanic". We will need to know where their roots are from.

Reason for Death: ____

Occupation/Trade: _______________________________ State/Country of death: _______________

~~~~~~

Was this person ever diagnosed with Cancer? _________

If so, at what age was the first diagnosis? _______

Type of Cancer:

BREAST   OVARIAN   COLON   PROSTATE   MELANOMA   ________________

LUNG   NON-HODGKIN LYMPHOMA   PANCREATIC   LEUKEMIA

What was the prognosis and treatment? Was treatment successful?

____

Was Genetic testing done and if so, were any mutations found that would indicate a higher chance of cancer? ____

Is there an occurrence of Ashkenazi Jewish ancestry? YES / NO

If yes, which family member does it originate from? ____________________________
~~~~~~

Please check below if any of these conditions apply. For each check, please use the additional space for explanations. Things like age when diagnosed and severity are helpful.

<table>
<tr><td>♡ ARTHRITIS</td><td>♡ HEARING LOSS</td></tr>
<tr><td>♡ BIRTH DEFECTS</td><td>♡ HIGH BLOOD PRESSURE</td></tr>
<tr><td>♡ HIGH CHOLESTROL</td><td>♡ PHYSICAL ABNORMALITIES</td></tr>
<tr><td>♡ MENTAL RETARDATION</td><td>♡ STROKE</td></tr>
<tr><td>♡ CLINICAL DEPRESSION</td><td>♡ VISION LOSS</td></tr>
<tr><td>♡ MULTIPLE MISCARRIGAGES</td><td>♡ ASTHMA</td></tr>
<tr><td>♡ OBESITY</td><td>♡ DIABETES</td></tr>
<tr><td>♡ OSTEOPOROSIS</td><td>♡ HEART DISEASE</td></tr>
<tr><td>♡ INFERTILITY</td><td>♡ VERY TALL OR VERY SHORT STATURE</td></tr>
<tr><td>♡ EARLY/DELAYED PUBERTY</td><td>*Compared to the rest of the family</td></tr>
<tr><td>♡ SPECTRUM/AUTISM</td><td>♡ BIRTH MARKS</td></tr>
<tr><td>♡ LUNG DISEASE</td><td>♡ BLOOD CLOTTING DISORDERS</td></tr>
<tr><td>♡ KIDNEY DISEASE</td><td>♡ ALZHEIMER'S/DIMENTIA</td></tr>
<tr><td>♡ ALLERGIES TO MEDICATIONS</td><td>♡ GOUT</td></tr>
</table>

NAME: ____

Date of Birth: _________   Date of Death: _________   State/country of birth: _______________

Part of a multiple birth? YES / NO

Spouse: _______________________________   Relation to main subject: _______________

Mother/Father of: _______________________________Child of: _______________________________

Ethnic Origin: ____

*For Ethnicity, please use "Irish, German, English", not "White" or use "Argentinian, Spanish, Brazilian", not "Hispanic". We will need to know where their roots are from.

Reason for Death: ____

Occupation/Trade: _______________________________   State/Country of death: _______________

~~~~~~

Was this person ever diagnosed with Cancer? _________

If so, at what age was the first diagnosis? _______

Type of Cancer:

BREAST   OVARIAN   COLON   PROSTATE   MELANOMA   _______________

LUNG   NON-HODGKIN LYMPHOMA   PANCREATIC   LEUKEMIA

What was the prognosis and treatment? Was treatment successful?

____

Was Genetic testing done and if so, were any mutations found that would indicate a higher chance of cancer? ____

Is there an occurrence of Ashkenazi Jewish ancestry? YES / NO

If yes, which family member does it originate from? _______________________
~~~~~~

Please check below if any of these conditions apply. For each check, please use the additional space for explanations. Things like age when diagnosed and severity are helpful.

♡ ARTHRITIS
♡ BIRTH DEFECTS
♡ HIGH CHOLESTROL
♡ MENTAL RETARDATION
♡ CLINICAL DEPRESSION
♡ MULTIPLE MISCARRIGAGES
♡ OBESITY
♡ OSTEOPOROSIS
♡ INFERTILITY
♡ EARLY/DELAYED PUBERTY
♡ SPECTRUM/AUTISM
♡ LUNG DISEASE
♡ KIDNEY DISEASE
♡ ALLERGIES TO MEDICATIONS

♡ HEARING LOSS
♡ HIGH BLOOD PRESSURE
♡ PHYSICAL ABNORMALITIES
♡ STROKE
♡ VISION LOSS
♡ ASTHMA
♡ DIABETES
♡ HEART DISEASE
♡ VERY TALL OR VERY SHORT STATURE
    *Compared to the rest of the family
♡ BIRTH MARKS
♡ BLOOD CLOTTING DISORDERS
♡ ALZHEIMER'S/DIMENTIA
♡ GOUT

NAME: ____

Date of Birth: __________   Date of Death: __________   State/country of birth: ____________________

Part of a multiple birth? YES / NO

Spouse: _______________________________   Relation to main subject: ____________________

Mother/Father of: _________________________________Child of: ____________________________________

Ethnic Origin: ____

*For Ethnicity, please use "Irish, German, English", not "White" or use "Argentinian, Spanish, Brazilian", not "Hispanic". We will need to know where their roots are from.

Reason for Death: ____

Occupation/Trade: ___________________________________   State/Country of death: ________________

~~~~~~

Was this person ever diagnosed with Cancer? __________

If so, at what age was the first diagnosis? ______

Type of Cancer:

BREAST   OVARIAN   COLON   PROSTATE   MELANOMA   __________________

LUNG   NON-HODGKIN LYMPHOMA   PANCREATIC   LEUKEMIA

What was the prognosis and treatment? Was treatment successful?

____

Was Genetic testing done and if so, were any mutations found that would indicate a higher chance of cancer? ____

Is there an occurrence of Ashkenazi Jewish ancestry? YES / NO

If yes, which family member does it originate from? ____________________
~~~~~~

Please check below if any of these conditions apply. For each check, please use the additional space for explanations. Things like age when diagnosed and severity are helpful.

♡ ARTHRITIS
♡ BIRTH DEFECTS
♡ HIGH CHOLESTROL
♡ MENTAL RETARDATION
♡ CLINICAL DEPRESSION
♡ MULTIPLE MISCARRIGAGES
♡ OBESITY
♡ OSTEOPOROSIS
♡ INFERTILITY
♡ EARLY/DELAYED PUBERTY
♡ SPECTRUM/AUTISM
♡ LUNG DISEASE
♡ KIDNEY DISEASE
♡ ALLERGIES TO MEDICATIONS

♡ HEARING LOSS
♡ HIGH BLOOD PRESSURE
♡ PHYSICAL ABNORMALITIES
♡ STROKE
♡ VISION LOSS
♡ ASTHMA
♡ DIABETES
♡ HEART DISEASE
♡ VERY TALL OR VERY SHORT STATURE
    *Compared to the rest of the family
♡ BIRTH MARKS
♡ BLOOD CLOTTING DISORDERS
♡ ALZHEIMER'S/DIMENTIA
♡ GOUT

NAME: _______________________________________

Date of Birth: _________   Date of Death: _________   State/country of birth: _______________

Part of a multiple birth? YES / NO

Spouse: _______________________________   Relation to main subject: _________________

Mother/Father of: _______________________________Child of: _______________________________

Ethnic Origin: ____

*For Ethnicity, please use "Irish, German, English", not "White" or use "Argentinian, Spanish, Brazilian", not "Hispanic". We will need to know where their roots are from.

Reason for Death: ____

Occupation/Trade: _______________________________   State/Country of death: _______________

~~~~~~

Was this person ever diagnosed with Cancer? _________

If so, at what age was the first diagnosis? _______

Type of Cancer:

BREAST   OVARIAN   COLON   PROSTATE   MELANOMA   _______________

LUNG   NON-HODGKIN LYMPHOMA   PANCREATIC   LEUKEMIA

What was the prognosis and treatment? Was treatment successful?

____

Was Genetic testing done and if so, were any mutations found that would indicate a higher chance of cancer? ____

Is there an occurrence of Ashkenazi Jewish ancestry? YES / NO

If yes, which family member does it originate from? _________________
~~~~~~

Please check below if any of these conditions apply. For each check, please use the additional space for explanations. Things like age when diagnosed and severity are helpful.

- ♡ ARTHRITIS
- ♡ BIRTH DEFECTS
- ♡ HIGH CHOLESTROL
- ♡ MENTAL RETARDATION
- ♡ CLINICAL DEPRESSION
- ♡ MULTIPLE MISCARRIGAGES
- ♡ OBESITY
- ♡ OSTEOPOROSIS
- ♡ INFERTILITY
- ♡ EARLY/DELAYED PUBERTY
- ♡ SPECTRUM/AUTISM
- ♡ LUNG DISEASE
- ♡ KIDNEY DISEASE
- ♡ ALLERGIES TO MEDICATIONS

- ♡ HEARING LOSS
- ♡ HIGH BLOOD PRESSURE
- ♡ PHYSICAL ABNORMALITIES
- ♡ STROKE
- ♡ VISION LOSS
- ♡ ASTHMA
- ♡ DIABETES
- ♡ HEART DISEASE
- ♡ VERY TALL OR VERY SHORT STATURE
      *Compared to the rest of the family
- ♡ BIRTH MARKS
- ♡ BLOOD CLOTTING DISORDERS
- ♡ ALZHEIMER'S/DIMENTIA
- ♡ GOUT

NAME: ____

Date of Birth: _________   Date of Death: _________   State/country of birth: ___________________

Part of a multiple birth? YES / NO

Spouse: _______________________________   Relation to main subject: __________________

Mother/Father of: _______________________________Child of: _______________________________

Ethnic Origin: ____

*For Ethnicity, please use "Irish, German, English", not "White" or use "Argentinian, Spanish, Brazilian", not "Hispanic". We will need to know where their roots are from.

Reason for Death: ____

Occupation/Trade: _______________________________   State/Country of death: ______________

~~~~~~

Was this person ever diagnosed with Cancer? _________

If so, at what age was the first diagnosis? _______

Type of Cancer:

BREAST   OVARIAN   COLON   PROSTATE   MELANOMA   ________________

LUNG   NON-HODGKIN LYMPHOMA   PANCREATIC   LEUKEMIA

What was the prognosis and treatment? Was treatment successful?

____

Was Genetic testing done and if so, were any mutations found that would indicate a higher chance of cancer? ____

Is there an occurrence of Ashkenazi Jewish ancestry? YES / NO

If yes, which family member does it originate from? ____________________
~~~~~~

Please check below if any of these conditions apply. For each check, please use the additional space for explanations. Things like age when diagnosed and severity are helpful.

♡ ARTHRITIS
♡ BIRTH DEFECTS
♡ HIGH CHOLESTROL
♡ MENTAL RETARDATION
♡ CLINICAL DEPRESSION
♡ MULTIPLE MISCARRIGAGES
♡ OBESITY
♡ OSTEOPOROSIS
♡ INFERTILITY
♡ EARLY/DELAYED PUBERTY
♡ SPECTRUM/AUTISM
♡ LUNG DISEASE
♡ KIDNEY DISEASE
♡ ALLERGIES TO MEDICATIONS

♡ HEARING LOSS
♡ HIGH BLOOD PRESSURE
♡ PHYSICAL ABNORMALITIES
♡ STROKE
♡ VISION LOSS
♡ ASTHMA
♡ DIABETES
♡ HEART DISEASE
♡ VERY TALL OR VERY SHORT STATURE
    *Compared to the rest of the family
♡ BIRTH MARKS
♡ BLOOD CLOTTING DISORDERS
♡ ALZHEIMER'S/DIMENTIA
♡ GOUT

NAME: ____

Date of Birth: _________ Date of Death: _________ State/country of birth: ___________________

Part of a multiple birth? YES / NO

Spouse: _______________________________ Relation to main subject: _________________

Mother/Father of: _______________________________Child of: _______________________________

Ethnic Origin: ____

*For Ethnicity, please use "Irish, German, English", not "White" or use "Argentinian, Spanish, Brazilian", not "Hispanic". We will need to know where their roots are from.

Reason for Death: ____

Occupation/Trade: _______________________________ State/Country of death: ________________

~~~~~~

Was this person ever diagnosed with Cancer? _________

If so, at what age was the first diagnosis? ______

Type of Cancer:

BREAST   OVARIAN   COLON   PROSTATE   MELANOMA   ____________________

LUNG   NON-HODGKIN LYMPHOMA   PANCREATIC   LEUKEMIA

What was the prognosis and treatment? Was treatment successful?

____

Was Genetic testing done and if so, were any mutations found that would indicate a higher chance of cancer? ____

Is there an occurrence of Ashkenazi Jewish ancestry? YES / NO

If yes, which family member does it originate from? ______________________________
~~~~~~

Please check below if any of these conditions apply. For each check, please use the additional space for explanations. Things like age when diagnosed and severity are helpful.

♡ ARTHRITIS
♡ BIRTH DEFECTS
♡ HIGH CHOLESTROL
♡ MENTAL RETARDATION
♡ CLINICAL DEPRESSION
♡ MULTIPLE MISCARRIGAGES
♡ OBESITY
♡ OSTEOPOROSIS
♡ INFERTILITY
♡ EARLY/DELAYED PUBERTY
♡ SPECTRUM/AUTISM
♡ LUNG DISEASE
♡ KIDNEY DISEASE
♡ ALLERGIES TO MEDICATIONS

♡ HEARING LOSS
♡ HIGH BLOOD PRESSURE
♡ PHYSICAL ABNORMALITIES
♡ STROKE
♡ VISION LOSS
♡ ASTHMA
♡ DIABETES
♡ HEART DISEASE
♡ VERY TALL OR VERY SHORT STATURE
        *Compared to the rest of the family
♡ BIRTH MARKS
♡ BLOOD CLOTTING DISORDERS
♡ ALZHEIMER'S/DIMENTIA
♡ GOUT

NAME: ____

Date of Birth: _________ Date of Death: _________ State/country of birth: _______________________

Part of a multiple birth? YES / NO

Spouse: _______________________________ Relation to main subject: _____________________

Mother/Father of: _______________________________Child of: _______________________________

Ethnic Origin: ____

*For Ethnicity, please use "Irish, German, English", not "White" or use "Argentinian, Spanish, Brazilian", not "Hispanic". We will need to know where their roots are from.

Reason for Death: ____

Occupation/Trade: _______________________________ State/Country of death: _______________

~~~~~~

Was this person ever diagnosed with Cancer? _________

If so, at what age was the first diagnosis? _______

Type of Cancer:

BREAST   OVARIAN   COLON   PROSTATE   MELANOMA   ___________________

LUNG   NON-HODGKIN LYMPHOMA   PANCREATIC   LEUKEMIA

What was the prognosis and treatment? Was treatment successful?

____

Was Genetic testing done and if so, were any mutations found that would indicate a higher chance of cancer? ____

Is there an occurrence of Ashkenazi Jewish ancestry? YES / NO

If yes, which family member does it originate from? ____________________________
~~~~~~

Please check below if any of these conditions apply. For each check, please use the additional space for explanations. Things like age when diagnosed and severity are helpful.

♡ ARTHRITIS
♡ BIRTH DEFECTS
♡ HIGH CHOLESTROL
♡ MENTAL RETARDATION
♡ CLINICAL DEPRESSION
♡ MULTIPLE MISCARRIGAGES
♡ OBESITY
♡ OSTEOPOROSIS
♡ INFERTILITY
♡ EARLY/DELAYED PUBERTY
♡ SPECTRUM/AUTISM
♡ LUNG DISEASE
♡ KIDNEY DISEASE
♡ ALLERGIES TO MEDICATIONS

♡ HEARING LOSS
♡ HIGH BLOOD PRESSURE
♡ PHYSICAL ABNORMALITIES
♡ STROKE
♡ VISION LOSS
♡ ASTHMA
♡ DIABETES
♡ HEART DISEASE
♡ VERY TALL OR VERY SHORT STATURE
    *Compared to the rest of the family
♡ BIRTH MARKS
♡ BLOOD CLOTTING DISORDERS
♡ ALZHEIMER'S/DIMENTIA
♡ GOUT

NAME: ____

Date of Birth: _________ Date of Death: _________ State/country of birth: ________________

Part of a multiple birth? YES / NO

Spouse: ______________________________ Relation to main subject: __________________

Mother/Father of: _______________________Child of: ______________________________

Ethnic Origin: ____

*For Ethnicity, please use "Irish, German, English", not "White" or use "Argentinian, Spanish, Brazilian", not "Hispanic". We will need to know where their roots are from.

Reason for Death: ____

Occupation/Trade: ____________________________ State/Country of death: ____________

~~~~~~

Was this person ever diagnosed with Cancer? _________

If so, at what age was the first diagnosis? ______

Type of Cancer:

BREAST   OVARIAN   COLON   PROSTATE   MELANOMA   ________________

LUNG   NON-HODGKIN LYMPHOMA   PANCREATIC   LEUKEMIA

What was the prognosis and treatment? Was treatment successful?

____

Was Genetic testing done and if so, were any mutations found that would indicate a higher chance of cancer? ____

Is there an occurrence of Ashkenazi Jewish ancestry? YES / NO

If yes, which family member does it originate from? ____________________________
~~~~~~

Please check below if any of these conditions apply. For each check, please use the additional space for explanations. Things like age when diagnosed and severity are helpful.

♡ ARTHRITIS	♡ HEARING LOSS
♡ BIRTH DEFECTS	♡ HIGH BLOOD PRESSURE
♡ HIGH CHOLESTROL	♡ PHYSICAL ABNORMALITIES
♡ MENTAL RETARDATION	♡ STROKE
♡ CLINICAL DEPRESSION	♡ VISION LOSS
♡ MULTIPLE MISCARRIGAGES	♡ ASTHMA
♡ OBESITY	♡ DIABETES
♡ OSTEOPOROSIS	♡ HEART DISEASE
♡ INFERTILITY	♡ VERY TALL OR VERY SHORT STATURE
♡ EARLY/DELAYED PUBERTY	*Compared to the rest of the family
♡ SPECTRUM/AUTISM	♡ BIRTH MARKS
♡ LUNG DISEASE	♡ BLOOD CLOTTING DISORDERS
♡ KIDNEY DISEASE	♡ ALZHEIMER'S/DIMENTIA
♡ ALLERGIES TO MEDICATIONS	♡ GOUT

NAME: ____

Date of Birth: _________ Date of Death: _________ State/country of birth: _______________

Part of a multiple birth? YES / NO

Spouse: _______________________________ Relation to main subject: _______________

Mother/Father of: _______________________Child of: _______________________

Ethnic Origin: ____

*For Ethnicity, please use "Irish, German, English", not "White" or use "Argentinian, Spanish, Brazilian", not "Hispanic". We will need to know where their roots are from.

Reason for Death: ____

Occupation/Trade: _______________________ State/Country of death: _______________

~~~~~~

Was this person ever diagnosed with Cancer? _________

If so, at what age was the first diagnosis? _______

Type of Cancer:

BREAST   OVARIAN   COLON   PROSTATE   MELANOMA   _______________

LUNG   NON-HODGKIN LYMPHOMA   PANCREATIC   LEUKEMIA

What was the prognosis and treatment? Was treatment successful?

____

Was Genetic testing done and if so, were any mutations found that would indicate a higher chance of cancer? ____

Is there an occurrence of Ashkenazi Jewish ancestry? YES / NO

If yes, which family member does it originate from? _______________________
~~~~~~

Please check below if any of these conditions apply. For each check, please use the additional space for explanations. Things like age when diagnosed and severity are helpful.

♡ ARTHRITIS	♡ HEARING LOSS
♡ BIRTH DEFECTS	♡ HIGH BLOOD PRESSURE
♡ HIGH CHOLESTROL	♡ PHYSICAL ABNORMALITIES
♡ MENTAL RETARDATION	♡ STROKE
♡ CLINICAL DEPRESSION	♡ VISION LOSS
♡ MULTIPLE MISCARRIGAGES	♡ ASTHMA
♡ OBESITY	♡ DIABETES
♡ OSTEOPOROSIS	♡ HEART DISEASE
♡ INFERTILITY	♡ VERY TALL OR VERY SHORT STATURE
♡ EARLY/DELAYED PUBERTY	*Compared to the rest of the family
♡ SPECTRUM/AUTISM	♡ BIRTH MARKS
♡ LUNG DISEASE	♡ BLOOD CLOTTING DISORDERS
♡ KIDNEY DISEASE	♡ ALZHEIMER'S/DIMENTIA
♡ ALLERGIES TO MEDICATIONS	♡ GOUT

NAME: ____

Date of Birth: _________ Date of Death: _________ State/country of birth: ___________________

Part of a multiple birth? YES / NO

Spouse: _______________________________ Relation to main subject: _____________________

Mother/Father of: ______________________________Child of: ___________________________

Ethnic Origin: ____

*For Ethnicity, please use "Irish, German, English", not "White" or use "Argentinian, Spanish, Brazilian", not "Hispanic". We will need to know where their roots are from.

Reason for Death: ____

Occupation/Trade: _______________________________ State/Country of death: ______________

~~~~~~

Was this person ever diagnosed with Cancer? _________

If so, at what age was the first diagnosis? _______

Type of Cancer:

BREAST   OVARIAN   COLON   PROSTATE   MELANOMA   _________________

LUNG   NON-HODGKIN LYMPHOMA   PANCREATIC   LEUKEMIA

What was the prognosis and treatment? Was treatment successful?

____

Was Genetic testing done and if so, were any mutations found that would indicate a higher chance of cancer? ____

Is there an occurrence of Ashkenazi Jewish ancestry? YES / NO

If yes, which family member does it originate from? ___________________________
~~~~~~

Please check below if any of these conditions apply. For each check, please use the additional space for explanations. Things like age when diagnosed and severity are helpful.

♡ ARTHRITIS
♡ BIRTH DEFECTS
♡ HIGH CHOLESTROL
♡ MENTAL RETARDATION
♡ CLINICAL DEPRESSION
♡ MULTIPLE MISCARRIGAGES
♡ OBESITY
♡ OSTEOPOROSIS
♡ INFERTILITY
♡ EARLY/DELAYED PUBERTY
♡ SPECTRUM/AUTISM
♡ LUNG DISEASE
♡ KIDNEY DISEASE
♡ ALLERGIES TO MEDICATIONS

♡ HEARING LOSS
♡ HIGH BLOOD PRESSURE
♡ PHYSICAL ABNORMALITIES
♡ STROKE
♡ VISION LOSS
♡ ASTHMA
♡ DIABETES
♡ HEART DISEASE
♡ VERY TALL OR VERY SHORT STATURE
    *Compared to the rest of the family
♡ BIRTH MARKS
♡ BLOOD CLOTTING DISORDERS
♡ ALZHEIMER'S/DIMENTIA
♡ GOUT

NAME: ____

Date of Birth: _________ Date of Death: _________ State/country of birth: ___________________

Part of a multiple birth? YES / NO

Spouse: _______________________________ Relation to main subject: ___________________

Mother/Father of: ______________________________Child of: ______________________________

Ethnic Origin: ____

*For Ethnicity, please use "Irish, German, English", not "White" or use "Argentinian, Spanish, Brazilian", not "Hispanic". We will need to know where their roots are from.

Reason for Death: ____

Occupation/Trade: _________________________________ State/Country of death: _____________

~~~~~~

Was this person ever diagnosed with Cancer? _________

If so, at what age was the first diagnosis? _______

Type of Cancer:

BREAST   OVARIAN   COLON   PROSTATE   MELANOMA   _________________

LUNG   NON-HODGKIN LYMPHOMA   PANCREATIC   LEUKEMIA

What was the prognosis and treatment? Was treatment successful?

____

Was Genetic testing done and if so, were any mutations found that would indicate a higher chance of cancer? ____

Is there an occurrence of Ashkenazi Jewish ancestry? YES / NO

If yes, which family member does it originate from? ___________________
~~~~~~

Please check below if any of these conditions apply. For each check, please use the additional space for explanations. Things like age when diagnosed and severity are helpful.

- ♡ ARTHRITIS
- ♡ BIRTH DEFECTS
- ♡ HIGH CHOLESTROL
- ♡ MENTAL RETARDATION
- ♡ CLINICAL DEPRESSION
- ♡ MULTIPLE MISCARRIGAGES
- ♡ OBESITY
- ♡ OSTEOPOROSIS
- ♡ INFERTILITY
- ♡ EARLY/DELAYED PUBERTY
- ♡ SPECTRUM/AUTISM
- ♡ LUNG DISEASE
- ♡ KIDNEY DISEASE
- ♡ ALLERGIES TO MEDICATIONS

- ♡ HEARING LOSS
- ♡ HIGH BLOOD PRESSURE
- ♡ PHYSICAL ABNORMALITIES
- ♡ STROKE
- ♡ VISION LOSS
- ♡ ASTHMA
- ♡ DIABETES
- ♡ HEART DISEASE
- ♡ VERY TALL OR VERY SHORT STATURE
     *Compared to the rest of the family
- ♡ BIRTH MARKS
- ♡ BLOOD CLOTTING DISORDERS
- ♡ ALZHEIMER'S/DIMENTIA
- ♡ GOUT

NAME: ____

Date of Birth: _________ Date of Death: _________ State/country of birth: __________________

Part of a multiple birth? YES / NO

Spouse: _______________________________ Relation to main subject: _________________

Mother/Father of: ________________________________Child of: __________________________

Ethnic Origin: ____

*For Ethnicity, please use "Irish, German, English", not "White" or use "Argentinian, Spanish, Brazilian", not "Hispanic". We will need to know where their roots are from.

Reason for Death: ____

Occupation/Trade: _______________________________ State/Country of death: _______________

~~~~~~

Was this person ever diagnosed with Cancer? _________

If so, at what age was the first diagnosis? _______

Type of Cancer:

BREAST   OVARIAN   COLON   PROSTATE   MELANOMA   ____________________

LUNG   NON-HODGKIN LYMPHOMA   PANCREATIC   LEUKEMIA

What was the prognosis and treatment? Was treatment successful?

____

Was Genetic testing done and if so, were any mutations found that would indicate a higher chance of cancer? ____

Is there an occurrence of Ashkenazi Jewish ancestry? YES / NO

If yes, which family member does it originate from? ____________________
~~~~~~

Please check below if any of these conditions apply. For each check, please use the additional space for explanations. Things like age when diagnosed and severity are helpful.

- ♡ ARTHRITIS
- ♡ BIRTH DEFECTS
- ♡ HIGH CHOLESTROL
- ♡ MENTAL RETARDATION
- ♡ CLINICAL DEPRESSION
- ♡ MULTIPLE MISCARRIGAGES
- ♡ OBESITY
- ♡ OSTEOPOROSIS
- ♡ INFERTILITY
- ♡ EARLY/DELAYED PUBERTY
- ♡ SPECTRUM/AUTISM
- ♡ LUNG DISEASE
- ♡ KIDNEY DISEASE
- ♡ ALLERGIES TO MEDICATIONS

- ♡ HEARING LOSS
- ♡ HIGH BLOOD PRESSURE
- ♡ PHYSICAL ABNORMALITIES
- ♡ STROKE
- ♡ VISION LOSS
- ♡ ASTHMA
- ♡ DIABETES
- ♡ HEART DISEASE
- ♡ VERY TALL OR VERY SHORT STATURE
      *Compared to the rest of the family
- ♡ BIRTH MARKS
- ♡ BLOOD CLOTTING DISORDERS
- ♡ ALZHEIMER'S/DIMENTIA
- ♡ GOUT

NAME: ____

Date of Birth: _________ Date of Death: _________ State/country of birth: ____________________

Part of a multiple birth? YES / NO

Spouse: ______________________________ Relation to main subject: __________________

Mother/Father of: _______________________________Child of: _______________________________

Ethnic Origin: ____

*For Ethnicity, please use "Irish, German, English", not "White" or use "Argentinian, Spanish, Brazilian", not "Hispanic". We will need to know where their roots are from.

Reason for Death: ____

Occupation/Trade: ______________________________ State/Country of death: ________________

~~~~~~

Was this person ever diagnosed with Cancer? _________

If so, at what age was the first diagnosis? ______

Type of Cancer:

BREAST   OVARIAN   COLON   PROSTATE   MELANOMA   ___________________

LUNG   NON-HODGKIN LYMPHOMA   PANCREATIC   LEUKEMIA

What was the prognosis and treatment? Was treatment successful?

____

Was Genetic testing done and if so, were any mutations found that would indicate a higher chance of cancer? ____

Is there an occurrence of Ashkenazi Jewish ancestry? YES / NO

If yes, which family member does it originate from? __________________
~~~~~~

Please check below if any of these conditions apply. For each check, please use the additional space for explanations. Things like age when diagnosed and severity are helpful.

♡ ARTHRITIS
♡ BIRTH DEFECTS
♡ HIGH CHOLESTROL
♡ MENTAL RETARDATION
♡ CLINICAL DEPRESSION
♡ MULTIPLE MISCARRIGAGES
♡ OBESITY
♡ OSTEOPOROSIS
♡ INFERTILITY
♡ EARLY/DELAYED PUBERTY
♡ SPECTRUM/AUTISM
♡ LUNG DISEASE
♡ KIDNEY DISEASE
♡ ALLERGIES TO MEDICATIONS

♡ HEARING LOSS
♡ HIGH BLOOD PRESSURE
♡ PHYSICAL ABNORMALITIES
♡ STROKE
♡ VISION LOSS
♡ ASTHMA
♡ DIABETES
♡ HEART DISEASE
♡ VERY TALL OR VERY SHORT STATURE
    *Compared to the rest of the family
♡ BIRTH MARKS
♡ BLOOD CLOTTING DISORDERS
♡ ALZHEIMER'S/DIMENTIA
♡ GOUT

NAME: ____

Date of Birth: __________ Date of Death: __________ State/country of birth: ___________________

Part of a multiple birth? YES / NO

Spouse: ______________________________ Relation to main subject: ___________________

Mother/Father of: ______________________________ Child of: ______________________________

Ethnic Origin: ____

*For Ethnicity, please use "Irish, German, English", not "White" or use "Argentinian, Spanish, Brazilian", not "Hispanic". We will need to know where their roots are from.

Reason for Death: ____

Occupation/Trade: ______________________________ State/Country of death: ________________

~~~~~~

Was this person ever diagnosed with Cancer? __________

If so, at what age was the first diagnosis? ______

Type of Cancer:

BREAST   OVARIAN   COLON   PROSTATE   MELANOMA   __________________

LUNG   NON-HODGKIN LYMPHOMA   PANCREATIC   LEUKEMIA

What was the prognosis and treatment? Was treatment successful?

____

Was Genetic testing done and if so, were any mutations found that would indicate a higher chance of cancer? ____

Is there an occurrence of Ashkenazi Jewish ancestry? YES / NO

If yes, which family member does it originate from? ___________________
~~~~~~

Please check below if any of these conditions apply. For each check, please use the additional space for explanations. Things like age when diagnosed and severity are helpful.

♡ ARTHRITIS
♡ BIRTH DEFECTS
♡ HIGH CHOLESTROL
♡ MENTAL RETARDATION
♡ CLINICAL DEPRESSION
♡ MULTIPLE MISCARRIGAGES
♡ OBESITY
♡ OSTEOPOROSIS
♡ INFERTILITY
♡ EARLY/DELAYED PUBERTY
♡ SPECTRUM/AUTISM
♡ LUNG DISEASE
♡ KIDNEY DISEASE
♡ ALLERGIES TO MEDICATIONS

♡ HEARING LOSS
♡ HIGH BLOOD PRESSURE
♡ PHYSICAL ABNORMALITIES
♡ STROKE
♡ VISION LOSS
♡ ASTHMA
♡ DIABETES
♡ HEART DISEASE
♡ VERY TALL OR VERY SHORT STATURE
    *Compared to the rest of the family
♡ BIRTH MARKS
♡ BLOOD CLOTTING DISORDERS
♡ ALZHEIMER'S/DIMENTIA
♡ GOUT

NAME: ____

Date of Birth: _________   Date of Death: _________ State/country of birth: _________________

Part of a multiple birth? YES / NO

Spouse: _______________________________   Relation to main subject: _________________

Mother/Father of: _______________________________Child of: _______________________________

Ethnic Origin: ____

*For Ethnicity, please use "Irish, German, English", not "White" or use "Argentinian, Spanish, Brazilian", not "Hispanic". We will need to know where their roots are from.

Reason for Death: ____

Occupation/Trade: _______________________________   State/Country of death: ______________

~~~~~~

Was this person ever diagnosed with Cancer? _________

If so, at what age was the first diagnosis? _______

Type of Cancer:

BREAST   OVARIAN   COLON   PROSTATE   MELANOMA   _________________

LUNG   NON-HODGKIN LYMPHOMA   PANCREATIC   LEUKEMIA

What was the prognosis and treatment? Was treatment successful?

____

Was Genetic testing done and if so, were any mutations found that would indicate a higher chance of cancer? ____

Is there an occurrence of Ashkenazi Jewish ancestry? YES / NO

If yes, which family member does it originate from? ___________________
~~~~~~

Please check below if any of these conditions apply. For each check, please use the additional space for explanations. Things like age when diagnosed and severity are helpful.

♡ ARTHRITIS	♡ HEARING LOSS
♡ BIRTH DEFECTS	♡ HIGH BLOOD PRESSURE
♡ HIGH CHOLESTROL	♡ PHYSICAL ABNORMALITIES
♡ MENTAL RETARDATION	♡ STROKE
♡ CLINICAL DEPRESSION	♡ VISION LOSS
♡ MULTIPLE MISCARRIGAGES	♡ ASTHMA
♡ OBESITY	♡ DIABETES
♡ OSTEOPOROSIS	♡ HEART DISEASE
♡ INFERTILITY	♡ VERY TALL OR VERY SHORT STATURE
♡ EARLY/DELAYED PUBERTY	*Compared to the rest of the family
♡ SPECTRUM/AUTISM	♡ BIRTH MARKS
♡ LUNG DISEASE	♡ BLOOD CLOTTING DISORDERS
♡ KIDNEY DISEASE	♡ ALZHEIMER'S/DIMENTIA
♡ ALLERGIES TO MEDICATIONS	♡ GOUT

NAME: ____

Date of Birth: _________ Date of Death: _________ State/country of birth: _________________

Part of a multiple birth? YES / NO

Spouse: _______________________________ Relation to main subject: _________________

Mother/Father of: ______________________________Child of: _____________________________

Ethnic Origin: ____

*For Ethnicity, please use "Irish, German, English", not "White" or use "Argentinian, Spanish, Brazilian", not "Hispanic". We will need to know where their roots are from.

Reason for Death: ____

Occupation/Trade: _______________________________ State/Country of death: ______________

~~~~~~

Was this person ever diagnosed with Cancer? _________

If so, at what age was the first diagnosis? ______

Type of Cancer:

BREAST   OVARIAN   COLON   PROSTATE   MELANOMA   ________________

LUNG   NON-HODGKIN LYMPHOMA   PANCREATIC   LEUKEMIA

What was the prognosis and treatment? Was treatment successful?

____

Was Genetic testing done and if so, were any mutations found that would indicate a higher chance of cancer? ____

Is there an occurrence of Ashkenazi Jewish ancestry? YES / NO

If yes, which family member does it originate from? ____________________________
~~~~~~

Please check below if any of these conditions apply. For each check, please use the additional space for explanations. Things like age when diagnosed and severity are helpful.

- ♡ ARTHRITIS
- ♡ BIRTH DEFECTS
- ♡ HIGH CHOLESTROL
- ♡ MENTAL RETARDATION
- ♡ CLINICAL DEPRESSION
- ♡ MULTIPLE MISCARRIGAGES
- ♡ OBESITY
- ♡ OSTEOPOROSIS
- ♡ INFERTILITY
- ♡ EARLY/DELAYED PUBERTY
- ♡ SPECTRUM/AUTISM
- ♡ LUNG DISEASE
- ♡ KIDNEY DISEASE
- ♡ ALLERGIES TO MEDICATIONS

- ♡ HEARING LOSS
- ♡ HIGH BLOOD PRESSURE
- ♡ PHYSICAL ABNORMALITIES
- ♡ STROKE
- ♡ VISION LOSS
- ♡ ASTHMA
- ♡ DIABETES
- ♡ HEART DISEASE
- ♡ VERY TALL OR VERY SHORT STATURE
     *Compared to the rest of the family
- ♡ BIRTH MARKS
- ♡ BLOOD CLOTTING DISORDERS
- ♡ ALZHEIMER'S/DIMENTIA
- ♡ GOUT

NAME: ____

Date of Birth: _________ Date of Death: _________ State/country of birth: _________________

Part of a multiple birth? YES / NO

Spouse: _______________________________ Relation to main subject: _________________

Mother/Father of: ____________________________Child of: _______________________________

Ethnic Origin: ____

*For Ethnicity, please use "Irish, German, English", not "White" or use "Argentinian, Spanish, Brazilian", not "Hispanic". We will need to know where their roots are from.

Reason for Death: ____

Occupation/Trade: ______________________________ State/Country of death: ______________

~~~~~~

Was this person ever diagnosed with Cancer? _________

If so, at what age was the first diagnosis? _______

Type of Cancer:

BREAST   OVARIAN   COLON   PROSTATE   MELANOMA   ____________________

LUNG   NON-HODGKIN LYMPHOMA   PANCREATIC   LEUKEMIA

What was the prognosis and treatment? Was treatment successful?

____

Was Genetic testing done and if so, were any mutations found that would indicate a higher chance of cancer? ____

Is there an occurrence of Ashkenazi Jewish ancestry? YES / NO

If yes, which family member does it originate from? ______________________
~~~~~~

Please check below if any of these conditions apply. For each check, please use the additional space for explanations. Things like age when diagnosed and severity are helpful.

- ♡ ARTHRITIS
- ♡ BIRTH DEFECTS
- ♡ HIGH CHOLESTROL
- ♡ MENTAL RETARDATION
- ♡ CLINICAL DEPRESSION
- ♡ MULTIPLE MISCARRIGAGES
- ♡ OBESITY
- ♡ OSTEOPOROSIS
- ♡ INFERTILITY
- ♡ EARLY/DELAYED PUBERTY
- ♡ SPECTRUM/AUTISM
- ♡ LUNG DISEASE
- ♡ KIDNEY DISEASE
- ♡ ALLERGIES TO MEDICATIONS
- ♡ HEARING LOSS
- ♡ HIGH BLOOD PRESSURE
- ♡ PHYSICAL ABNORMALITIES
- ♡ STROKE
- ♡ VISION LOSS
- ♡ ASTHMA
- ♡ DIABETES
- ♡ HEART DISEASE
- ♡ VERY TALL OR VERY SHORT STATURE
  *Compared to the rest of the family
- ♡ BIRTH MARKS
- ♡ BLOOD CLOTTING DISORDERS
- ♡ ALZHEIMER'S/DIMENTIA
- ♡ GOUT

NAME: ____

Date of Birth: __________ Date of Death: __________ State/country of birth: ___________________

Part of a multiple birth? YES / NO

Spouse: ______________________________ Relation to main subject: ___________________

Mother/Father of: ______________________________Child of: ___________________________

Ethnic Origin: ____

*For Ethnicity, please use "Irish, German, English", not "White" or use "Argentinian, Spanish, Brazilian", not "Hispanic". We will need to know where their roots are from.

Reason for Death: ____

Occupation/Trade: ______________________________ State/Country of death: _______________

~~~~~~

Was this person ever diagnosed with Cancer? __________

If so, at what age was the first diagnosis? _______

Type of Cancer:

BREAST   OVARIAN   COLON   PROSTATE   MELANOMA   ___________________

LUNG   NON-HODGKIN LYMPHOMA   PANCREATIC   LEUKEMIA

What was the prognosis and treatment? Was treatment successful?

____

Was Genetic testing done and if so, were any mutations found that would indicate a higher chance of cancer? ____

Is there an occurrence of Ashkenazi Jewish ancestry? YES / NO

If yes, which family member does it originate from? ___________________________
~~~~~~

Please check below if any of these conditions apply. For each check, please use the additional space for explanations. Things like age when diagnosed and severity are helpful.

- ♡ ARTHRITIS
- ♡ BIRTH DEFECTS
- ♡ HIGH CHOLESTROL
- ♡ MENTAL RETARDATION
- ♡ CLINICAL DEPRESSION
- ♡ MULTIPLE MISCARRIGAGES
- ♡ OBESITY
- ♡ OSTEOPOROSIS
- ♡ INFERTILITY
- ♡ EARLY/DELAYED PUBERTY
- ♡ SPECTRUM/AUTISM
- ♡ LUNG DISEASE
- ♡ KIDNEY DISEASE
- ♡ ALLERGIES TO MEDICATIONS

- ♡ HEARING LOSS
- ♡ HIGH BLOOD PRESSURE
- ♡ PHYSICAL ABNORMALITIES
- ♡ STROKE
- ♡ VISION LOSS
- ♡ ASTHMA
- ♡ DIABETES
- ♡ HEART DISEASE
- ♡ VERY TALL OR VERY SHORT STATURE
    - *Compared to the rest of the family
- ♡ BIRTH MARKS
- ♡ BLOOD CLOTTING DISORDERS
- ♡ ALZHEIMER'S/DIMENTIA
- ♡ GOUT

NAME: _______________________________________

Date of Birth: _________ Date of Death: _________ State/country of birth: _______________

Part of a multiple birth? YES / NO

Spouse: _______________________________ Relation to main subject: _______________

Mother/Father of: ________________________Child of: ___________________________

Ethnic Origin: ____

*For Ethnicity, please use "Irish, German, English", not "White" or use "Argentinian, Spanish, Brazilian", not "Hispanic". We will need to know where their roots are from.

Reason for Death: ____

Occupation/Trade: ______________________________ State/Country of death: _____________

~~~~~~

Was this person ever diagnosed with Cancer? _________

If so, at what age was the first diagnosis? _______

Type of Cancer:

BREAST   OVARIAN   COLON   PROSTATE   MELANOMA   _______________

LUNG   NON-HODGKIN LYMPHOMA   PANCREATIC   LEUKEMIA

What was the prognosis and treatment? Was treatment successful?

____

Was Genetic testing done and if so, were any mutations found that would indicate a higher chance of cancer? ____

Is there an occurrence of Ashkenazi Jewish ancestry? YES / NO

If yes, which family member does it originate from? ___________________
~~~~~~

Please check below if any of these conditions apply. For each check, please use the additional space for explanations. Things like age when diagnosed and severity are helpful.

♡ ARTHRITIS
♡ BIRTH DEFECTS
♡ HIGH CHOLESTROL
♡ MENTAL RETARDATION
♡ CLINICAL DEPRESSION
♡ MULTIPLE MISCARRIGAGES
♡ OBESITY
♡ OSTEOPOROSIS
♡ INFERTILITY
♡ EARLY/DELAYED PUBERTY
♡ SPECTRUM/AUTISM
♡ LUNG DISEASE
♡ KIDNEY DISEASE
♡ ALLERGIES TO MEDICATIONS

♡ HEARING LOSS
♡ HIGH BLOOD PRESSURE
♡ PHYSICAL ABNORMALITIES
♡ STROKE
♡ VISION LOSS
♡ ASTHMA
♡ DIABETES
♡ HEART DISEASE
♡ VERY TALL OR VERY SHORT STATURE
        *Compared to the rest of the family
♡ BIRTH MARKS
♡ BLOOD CLOTTING DISORDERS
♡ ALZHEIMER'S/DIMENTIA
♡ GOUT

NAME: ____

Date of Birth: _________ Date of Death: _________ State/country of birth: ___________________

Part of a multiple birth? YES / NO

Spouse: ______________________________ Relation to main subject: ___________________

Mother/Father of: _______________________________Child of: _______________________________

Ethnic Origin: ____

*For Ethnicity, please use "Irish, German, English", not "White" or use "Argentinian, Spanish, Brazilian", not "Hispanic". We will need to know where their roots are from.

Reason for Death: ____

Occupation/Trade: ______________________________ State/Country of death: _______________

~~~~~~

Was this person ever diagnosed with Cancer? _________

If so, at what age was the first diagnosis? _______

Type of Cancer:

BREAST   OVARIAN   COLON   PROSTATE   MELANOMA   ________________

LUNG   NON-HODGKIN LYMPHOMA   PANCREATIC   LEUKEMIA

What was the prognosis and treatment? Was treatment successful?

____

Was Genetic testing done and if so, were any mutations found that would indicate a higher chance of cancer? ____

Is there an occurrence of Ashkenazi Jewish ancestry? YES / NO

If yes, which family member does it originate from? ___________________________
~~~~~~

Please check below if any of these conditions apply. For each check, please use the additional space for explanations. Things like age when diagnosed and severity are helpful.

♡ ARTHRITIS
♡ BIRTH DEFECTS
♡ HIGH CHOLESTROL
♡ MENTAL RETARDATION
♡ CLINICAL DEPRESSION
♡ MULTIPLE MISCARRIGAGES
♡ OBESITY
♡ OSTEOPOROSIS
♡ INFERTILITY
♡ EARLY/DELAYED PUBERTY
♡ SPECTRUM/AUTISM
♡ LUNG DISEASE
♡ KIDNEY DISEASE
♡ ALLERGIES TO MEDICATIONS

♡ HEARING LOSS
♡ HIGH BLOOD PRESSURE
♡ PHYSICAL ABNORMALITIES
♡ STROKE
♡ VISION LOSS
♡ ASTHMA
♡ DIABETES
♡ HEART DISEASE
♡ VERY TALL OR VERY SHORT STATURE
    *Compared to the rest of the family
♡ BIRTH MARKS
♡ BLOOD CLOTTING DISORDERS
♡ ALZHEIMER'S/DIMENTIA
♡ GOUT

NAME: ____

Date of Birth: _________ Date of Death: _________ State/country of birth: _________________

Part of a multiple birth? YES / NO

Spouse: _______________________________ Relation to main subject: __________________

Mother/Father of: ___________________________Child of: _______________________________

Ethnic Origin: ____

*For Ethnicity, please use "Irish, German, English", not "White" or use "Argentinian, Spanish, Brazilian", not "Hispanic". We will need to know where their roots are from.

Reason for Death: ____

Occupation/Trade: _________________________________ State/Country of death: _______________

~~~~~~

Was this person ever diagnosed with Cancer? _________

If so, at what age was the first diagnosis? _______

Type of Cancer:

BREAST   OVARIAN   COLON   PROSTATE   MELANOMA   ________________

LUNG   NON-HODGKIN LYMPHOMA   PANCREATIC   LEUKEMIA

What was the prognosis and treatment? Was treatment successful?

____

Was Genetic testing done and if so, were any mutations found that would indicate a higher chance of cancer? ____

Is there an occurrence of Ashkenazi Jewish ancestry? YES / NO

If yes, which family member does it originate from? ____________________________
~~~~~~

Please check below if any of these conditions apply. For each check, please use the additional space for explanations. Things like age when diagnosed and severity are helpful.

- ♡ ARTHRITIS
- ♡ BIRTH DEFECTS
- ♡ HIGH CHOLESTROL
- ♡ MENTAL RETARDATION
- ♡ CLINICAL DEPRESSION
- ♡ MULTIPLE MISCARRIGAGES
- ♡ OBESITY
- ♡ OSTEOPOROSIS
- ♡ INFERTILITY
- ♡ EARLY/DELAYED PUBERTY
- ♡ SPECTRUM/AUTISM
- ♡ LUNG DISEASE
- ♡ KIDNEY DISEASE
- ♡ ALLERGIES TO MEDICATIONS

- ♡ HEARING LOSS
- ♡ HIGH BLOOD PRESSURE
- ♡ PHYSICAL ABNORMALITIES
- ♡ STROKE
- ♡ VISION LOSS
- ♡ ASTHMA
- ♡ DIABETES
- ♡ HEART DISEASE
- ♡ VERY TALL OR VERY SHORT STATURE
      *Compared to the rest of the family
- ♡ BIRTH MARKS
- ♡ BLOOD CLOTTING DISORDERS
- ♡ ALZHEIMER'S/DIMENTIA
- ♡ GOUT

NAME: _______________________________________

Date of Birth: _________ Date of Death: _________ State/country of birth: ________________

Part of a multiple birth? YES / NO

Spouse: _______________________________ Relation to main subject: __________________

Mother/Father of: _______________________________Child of: _______________________________

Ethnic Origin: ____

*For Ethnicity, please use "Irish, German, English", not "White" or use "Argentinian, Spanish, Brazilian", not "Hispanic". We will need to know where their roots are from.

Reason for Death: ____

Occupation/Trade: _______________________________ State/Country of death: ______________

~~~~~~

Was this person ever diagnosed with Cancer? _________

If so, at what age was the first diagnosis? ______

Type of Cancer:

BREAST   OVARIAN   COLON   PROSTATE   MELANOMA   ____________________

LUNG   NON-HODGKIN LYMPHOMA   PANCREATIC   LEUKEMIA

What was the prognosis and treatment? Was treatment successful?

____

Was Genetic testing done and if so, were any mutations found that would indicate a higher chance of cancer? ____

Is there an occurrence of Ashkenazi Jewish ancestry? YES / NO

If yes, which family member does it originate from? ____________________
~~~~~~

Please check below if any of these conditions apply. For each check, please use the additional space for explanations. Things like age when diagnosed and severity are helpful.

♡ ARTHRITIS
♡ BIRTH DEFECTS
♡ HIGH CHOLESTROL
♡ MENTAL RETARDATION
♡ CLINICAL DEPRESSION
♡ MULTIPLE MISCARRIGAGES
♡ OBESITY
♡ OSTEOPOROSIS
♡ INFERTILITY
♡ EARLY/DELAYED PUBERTY
♡ SPECTRUM/AUTISM
♡ LUNG DISEASE
♡ KIDNEY DISEASE
♡ ALLERGIES TO MEDICATIONS

♡ HEARING LOSS
♡ HIGH BLOOD PRESSURE
♡ PHYSICAL ABNORMALITIES
♡ STROKE
♡ VISION LOSS
♡ ASTHMA
♡ DIABETES
♡ HEART DISEASE
♡ VERY TALL OR VERY SHORT STATURE
    *Compared to the rest of the family
♡ BIRTH MARKS
♡ BLOOD CLOTTING DISORDERS
♡ ALZHEIMER'S/DIMENTIA
♡ GOUT

NAME: ____

Date of Birth: _________ Date of Death: _________ State/country of birth: ________________

Part of a multiple birth? YES / NO

Spouse: _______________________________ Relation to main subject: ___________________

Mother/Father of: _______________________________Child of: _______________________________

Ethnic Origin: ____

*For Ethnicity, please use "Irish, German, English", not "White" or use "Argentinian, Spanish, Brazilian", not "Hispanic". We will need to know where their roots are from.

Reason for Death: ____

Occupation/Trade: _______________________________ State/Country of death: ______________

~~~~~~

Was this person ever diagnosed with Cancer? _________

If so, at what age was the first diagnosis? _______

Type of Cancer:

BREAST   OVARIAN   COLON   PROSTATE   MELANOMA   ________________

LUNG   NON-HODGKIN LYMPHOMA   PANCREATIC   LEUKEMIA

What was the prognosis and treatment? Was treatment successful?

____

Was Genetic testing done and if so, were any mutations found that would indicate a higher chance of cancer? ____

Is there an occurrence of Ashkenazi Jewish ancestry? YES / NO

If yes, which family member does it originate from? ___________________________
~~~~~~

Please check below if any of these conditions apply. For each check, please use the additional space for explanations. Things like age when diagnosed and severity are helpful.

♡ ARTHRITIS	♡ HEARING LOSS
♡ BIRTH DEFECTS	♡ HIGH BLOOD PRESSURE
♡ HIGH CHOLESTROL	♡ PHYSICAL ABNORMALITIES
♡ MENTAL RETARDATION	♡ STROKE
♡ CLINICAL DEPRESSION	♡ VISION LOSS
♡ MULTIPLE MISCARRIGAGES	♡ ASTHMA
♡ OBESITY	♡ DIABETES
♡ OSTEOPOROSIS	♡ HEART DISEASE
♡ INFERTILITY	♡ VERY TALL OR VERY SHORT STATURE
♡ EARLY/DELAYED PUBERTY	*Compared to the rest of the family
♡ SPECTRUM/AUTISM	♡ BIRTH MARKS
♡ LUNG DISEASE	♡ BLOOD CLOTTING DISORDERS
♡ KIDNEY DISEASE	♡ ALZHEIMER'S/DIMENTIA
♡ ALLERGIES TO MEDICATIONS	♡ GOUT

NAME: _______________________________________

Date of Birth: _________ Date of Death: _________ State/country of birth: ____________________

Part of a multiple birth? YES / NO

Spouse: _______________________________ Relation to main subject: ____________________

Mother/Father of: _______________________________Child of: ______________________________

Ethnic Origin: ____

*For Ethnicity, please use "Irish, German, English", not "White" or use "Argentinian, Spanish, Brazilian", not "Hispanic". We will need to know where their roots are from.

Reason for Death: ____

Occupation/Trade: ________________________________ State/Country of death: ______________

~~~~~~

Was this person ever diagnosed with Cancer? _________

If so, at what age was the first diagnosis? _______

Type of Cancer:

BREAST   OVARIAN   COLON   PROSTATE   MELANOMA   ________________

LUNG   NON-HODGKIN LYMPHOMA   PANCREATIC   LEUKEMIA

What was the prognosis and treatment? Was treatment successful?

____

Was Genetic testing done and if so, were any mutations found that would indicate a higher chance of cancer? ____

Is there an occurrence of Ashkenazi Jewish ancestry? YES / NO

If yes, which family member does it originate from? ____________________________
~~~~~~

Please check below if any of these conditions apply. For each check, please use the additional space for explanations. Things like age when diagnosed and severity are helpful.

♡ ARTHRITIS
♡ BIRTH DEFECTS
♡ HIGH CHOLESTROL
♡ MENTAL RETARDATION
♡ CLINICAL DEPRESSION
♡ MULTIPLE MISCARRIGAGES
♡ OBESITY
♡ OSTEOPOROSIS
♡ INFERTILITY
♡ EARLY/DELAYED PUBERTY
♡ SPECTRUM/AUTISM
♡ LUNG DISEASE
♡ KIDNEY DISEASE
♡ ALLERGIES TO MEDICATIONS

♡ HEARING LOSS
♡ HIGH BLOOD PRESSURE
♡ PHYSICAL ABNORMALITIES
♡ STROKE
♡ VISION LOSS
♡ ASTHMA
♡ DIABETES
♡ HEART DISEASE
♡ VERY TALL OR VERY SHORT STATURE
    *Compared to the rest of the family
♡ BIRTH MARKS
♡ BLOOD CLOTTING DISORDERS
♡ ALZHEIMER'S/DIMENTIA
♡ GOUT

NAME: ____

Date of Birth: _________   Date of Death: _________   State/country of birth: _______________________

Part of a multiple birth? YES / NO

Spouse: _______________________________   Relation to main subject: _____________________

Mother/Father of: _________________________Child of: _______________________________

Ethnic Origin: ____

*For Ethnicity, please use "Irish, German, English", not "White" or use "Argentinian, Spanish, Brazilian", not "Hispanic". We will need to know where their roots are from.

Reason for Death: ____

Occupation/Trade: _________________________________   State/Country of death: _______________

~~~~~~

Was this person ever diagnosed with Cancer? _________

If so, at what age was the first diagnosis? _______

Type of Cancer:

BREAST   OVARIAN   COLON   PROSTATE   MELANOMA   _________________

LUNG   NON-HODGKIN LYMPHOMA   PANCREATIC   LEUKEMIA

What was the prognosis and treatment? Was treatment successful?

____

Was Genetic testing done and if so, were any mutations found that would indicate a higher chance of cancer? ____

Is there an occurrence of Ashkenazi Jewish ancestry? YES / NO

If yes, which family member does it originate from? ____________________
~~~~~~

Please check below if any of these conditions apply. For each check, please use the additional space for explanations. Things like age when diagnosed and severity are helpful.

♡ ARTHRITIS
♡ BIRTH DEFECTS
♡ HIGH CHOLESTROL
♡ MENTAL RETARDATION
♡ CLINICAL DEPRESSION
♡ MULTIPLE MISCARRIGAGES
♡ OBESITY
♡ OSTEOPOROSIS
♡ INFERTILITY
♡ EARLY/DELAYED PUBERTY
♡ SPECTRUM/AUTISM
♡ LUNG DISEASE
♡ KIDNEY DISEASE
♡ ALLERGIES TO MEDICATIONS

♡ HEARING LOSS
♡ HIGH BLOOD PRESSURE
♡ PHYSICAL ABNORMALITIES
♡ STROKE
♡ VISION LOSS
♡ ASTHMA
♡ DIABETES
♡ HEART DISEASE
♡ VERY TALL OR VERY SHORT STATURE
   *Compared to the rest of the family
♡ BIRTH MARKS
♡ BLOOD CLOTTING DISORDERS
♡ ALZHEIMER'S/DIMENTIA
♡ GOUT

NAME: ____

Date of Birth: _________ Date of Death: _________ State/country of birth: ___________________

Part of a multiple birth? YES / NO

Spouse: _______________________________ Relation to main subject: ___________________

Mother/Father of: _______________________________Child of: _______________________________

Ethnic Origin: ____

*For Ethnicity, please use "Irish, German, English", not "White" or use "Argentinian, Spanish, Brazilian", not "Hispanic". We will need to know where their roots are from.

Reason for Death: ____

Occupation/Trade: _________________________________ State/Country of death: _______________

~~~~~~

Was this person ever diagnosed with Cancer? _________

If so, at what age was the first diagnosis? _______

Type of Cancer:

BREAST   OVARIAN   COLON   PROSTATE   MELANOMA   _________________

LUNG   NON-HODGKIN LYMPHOMA   PANCREATIC   LEUKEMIA

What was the prognosis and treatment? Was treatment successful?

____

Was Genetic testing done and if so, were any mutations found that would indicate a higher chance of cancer? ____

Is there an occurrence of Ashkenazi Jewish ancestry? YES / NO

If yes, which family member does it originate from? ___________________
~~~~~~

Please check below if any of these conditions apply. For each check, please use the additional space for explanations. Things like age when diagnosed and severity are helpful.

♡ ARTHRITIS
♡ BIRTH DEFECTS
♡ HIGH CHOLESTROL
♡ MENTAL RETARDATION
♡ CLINICAL DEPRESSION
♡ MULTIPLE MISCARRIGAGES
♡ OBESITY
♡ OSTEOPOROSIS
♡ INFERTILITY
♡ EARLY/DELAYED PUBERTY
♡ SPECTRUM/AUTISM
♡ LUNG DISEASE
♡ KIDNEY DISEASE
♡ ALLERGIES TO MEDICATIONS

♡ HEARING LOSS
♡ HIGH BLOOD PRESSURE
♡ PHYSICAL ABNORMALITIES
♡ STROKE
♡ VISION LOSS
♡ ASTHMA
♡ DIABETES
♡ HEART DISEASE
♡ VERY TALL OR VERY SHORT STATURE
    *Compared to the rest of the family
♡ BIRTH MARKS
♡ BLOOD CLOTTING DISORDERS
♡ ALZHEIMER'S/DIMENTIA
♡ GOUT

NAME: ____

Date of Birth: _________   Date of Death: _________ State/country of birth: ___________________

Part of a multiple birth? YES / NO

Spouse: _______________________________   Relation to main subject: ___________________

Mother/Father of: _________________________________Child of: ___________________________

Ethnic Origin: ____

*For Ethnicity, please use "Irish, German, English", not "White" or use "Argentinian, Spanish, Brazilian", not "Hispanic". We will need to know where their roots are from.

Reason for Death: ____

Occupation/Trade: _______________________________   State/Country of death: ______________

~~~~~~

Was this person ever diagnosed with Cancer? _________

If so, at what age was the first diagnosis? _______

Type of Cancer:

BREAST   OVARIAN   COLON   PROSTATE   MELANOMA   _________________

LUNG   NON-HODGKIN LYMPHOMA   PANCREATIC   LEUKEMIA

What was the prognosis and treatment? Was treatment successful?

____

Was Genetic testing done and if so, were any mutations found that would indicate a higher chance of cancer? ____

Is there an occurrence of Ashkenazi Jewish ancestry? YES / NO

If yes, which family member does it originate from? ___________________
~~~~~~

Please check below if any of these conditions apply. For each check, please use the additional space for explanations. Things like age when diagnosed and severity are helpful.

♡ ARTHRITIS
♡ BIRTH DEFECTS
♡ HIGH CHOLESTROL
♡ MENTAL RETARDATION
♡ CLINICAL DEPRESSION
♡ MULTIPLE MISCARRIGAGES
♡ OBESITY
♡ OSTEOPOROSIS
♡ INFERTILITY
♡ EARLY/DELAYED PUBERTY
♡ SPECTRUM/AUTISM
♡ LUNG DISEASE
♡ KIDNEY DISEASE
♡ ALLERGIES TO MEDICATIONS

♡ HEARING LOSS
♡ HIGH BLOOD PRESSURE
♡ PHYSICAL ABNORMALITIES
♡ STROKE
♡ VISION LOSS
♡ ASTHMA
♡ DIABETES
♡ HEART DISEASE
♡ VERY TALL OR VERY SHORT STATURE
    *Compared to the rest of the family
♡ BIRTH MARKS
♡ BLOOD CLOTTING DISORDERS
♡ ALZHEIMER'S/DIMENTIA
♡ GOUT

NAME: ____

Date of Birth: _________ Date of Death: _________ State/country of birth: ________________

Part of a multiple birth? YES / NO

Spouse: ______________________________ Relation to main subject: ____________________

Mother/Father of: ______________________________Child of: ____________________________

Ethnic Origin: ____

*For Ethnicity, please use "Irish, German, English", not "White" or use "Argentinian, Spanish, Brazilian", not "Hispanic". We will need to know where their roots are from.

Reason for Death: ____

Occupation/Trade: ______________________________ State/Country of death: ______________

~~~~~~

Was this person ever diagnosed with Cancer? _________

If so, at what age was the first diagnosis? _______

Type of Cancer:

BREAST   OVARIAN   COLON   PROSTATE   MELANOMA   ________________

LUNG   NON-HODGKIN LYMPHOMA   PANCREATIC   LEUKEMIA

What was the prognosis and treatment? Was treatment successful?

____

Was Genetic testing done and if so, were any mutations found that would indicate a higher chance of cancer? ____

Is there an occurrence of Ashkenazi Jewish ancestry? YES / NO

If yes, which family member does it originate from? ____________________
~~~~~~

Please check below if any of these conditions apply. For each check, please use the additional space for explanations. Things like age when diagnosed and severity are helpful.

- ♡ ARTHRITIS
- ♡ BIRTH DEFECTS
- ♡ HIGH CHOLESTROL
- ♡ MENTAL RETARDATION
- ♡ CLINICAL DEPRESSION
- ♡ MULTIPLE MISCARRIGAGES
- ♡ OBESITY
- ♡ OSTEOPOROSIS
- ♡ INFERTILITY
- ♡ EARLY/DELAYED PUBERTY
- ♡ SPECTRUM/AUTISM
- ♡ LUNG DISEASE
- ♡ KIDNEY DISEASE
- ♡ ALLERGIES TO MEDICATIONS

- ♡ HEARING LOSS
- ♡ HIGH BLOOD PRESSURE
- ♡ PHYSICAL ABNORMALITIES
- ♡ STROKE
- ♡ VISION LOSS
- ♡ ASTHMA
- ♡ DIABETES
- ♡ HEART DISEASE
- ♡ VERY TALL OR VERY SHORT STATURE
      *Compared to the rest of the family
- ♡ BIRTH MARKS
- ♡ BLOOD CLOTTING DISORDERS
- ♡ ALZHEIMER'S/DIMENTIA
- ♡ GOUT

NAME: ____

Date of Birth: _________ Date of Death: _________ State/country of birth: _______________

Part of a multiple birth? YES / NO

Spouse: _______________________________ Relation to main subject: _______________________

Mother/Father of: _______________________________Child of: _______________________________

Ethnic Origin: ____

*For Ethnicity, please use "Irish, German, English", not "White" or use "Argentinian, Spanish, Brazilian", not "Hispanic". We will need to know where their roots are from.

Reason for Death: ____

Occupation/Trade: _______________________________ State/Country of death: _______________

~~~~~~

Was this person ever diagnosed with Cancer? _________

If so, at what age was the first diagnosis? _______

Type of Cancer:

BREAST   OVARIAN   COLON   PROSTATE   MELANOMA   ________________

LUNG   NON-HODGKIN LYMPHOMA   PANCREATIC   LEUKEMIA

What was the prognosis and treatment? Was treatment successful?

____

Was Genetic testing done and if so, were any mutations found that would indicate a higher chance of cancer? ____

Is there an occurrence of Ashkenazi Jewish ancestry? YES / NO

If yes, which family member does it originate from? ___________________________
~~~~~~

Please check below if any of these conditions apply. For each check, please use the additional space for explanations. Things like age when diagnosed and severity are helpful.

♡ ARTHRITIS
♡ BIRTH DEFECTS
♡ HIGH CHOLESTROL
♡ MENTAL RETARDATION
♡ CLINICAL DEPRESSION
♡ MULTIPLE MISCARRIGAGES
♡ OBESITY
♡ OSTEOPOROSIS
♡ INFERTILITY
♡ EARLY/DELAYED PUBERTY
♡ SPECTRUM/AUTISM
♡ LUNG DISEASE
♡ KIDNEY DISEASE
♡ ALLERGIES TO MEDICATIONS

♡ HEARING LOSS
♡ HIGH BLOOD PRESSURE
♡ PHYSICAL ABNORMALITIES
♡ STROKE
♡ VISION LOSS
♡ ASTHMA
♡ DIABETES
♡ HEART DISEASE
♡ VERY TALL OR VERY SHORT STATURE
     *Compared to the rest of the family
♡ BIRTH MARKS
♡ BLOOD CLOTTING DISORDERS
♡ ALZHEIMER'S/DIMENTIA
♡ GOUT

NAME: ____

Date of Birth: _________ Date of Death: _________ State/country of birth: _______________

Part of a multiple birth? YES / NO

Spouse: ______________________________ Relation to main subject: ___________________

Mother/Father of: ______________________________Child of: _______________________________

Ethnic Origin: ____

*For Ethnicity, please use "Irish, German, English", not "White" or use "Argentinian, Spanish, Brazilian", not "Hispanic". We will need to know where their roots are from.

Reason for Death: ____

Occupation/Trade: ______________________________ State/Country of death: _______________

~~~~~~

Was this person ever diagnosed with Cancer? _________

If so, at what age was the first diagnosis? _______

Type of Cancer:

BREAST   OVARIAN   COLON   PROSTATE   MELANOMA   _________________

LUNG   NON-HODGKIN LYMPHOMA   PANCREATIC   LEUKEMIA

What was the prognosis and treatment? Was treatment successful?

____

Was Genetic testing done and if so, were any mutations found that would indicate a higher chance of cancer? ____

Is there an occurrence of Ashkenazi Jewish ancestry? YES / NO

If yes, which family member does it originate from? _____________________
~~~~~~

Please check below if any of these conditions apply. For each check, please use the additional space for explanations. Things like age when diagnosed and severity are helpful.

♡ ARTHRITIS
♡ BIRTH DEFECTS
♡ HIGH CHOLESTROL
♡ MENTAL RETARDATION
♡ CLINICAL DEPRESSION
♡ MULTIPLE MISCARRIGAGES
♡ OBESITY
♡ OSTEOPOROSIS
♡ INFERTILITY
♡ EARLY/DELAYED PUBERTY
♡ SPECTRUM/AUTISM
♡ LUNG DISEASE
♡ KIDNEY DISEASE
♡ ALLERGIES TO MEDICATIONS

♡ HEARING LOSS
♡ HIGH BLOOD PRESSURE
♡ PHYSICAL ABNORMALITIES
♡ STROKE
♡ VISION LOSS
♡ ASTHMA
♡ DIABETES
♡ HEART DISEASE
♡ VERY TALL OR VERY SHORT STATURE
        *Compared to the rest of the family
♡ BIRTH MARKS
♡ BLOOD CLOTTING DISORDERS
♡ ALZHEIMER'S/DIMENTIA
♡ GOUT

NAME: ____

Date of Birth: _________ Date of Death: _________ State/country of birth: _______________

Part of a multiple birth? YES / NO

Spouse: _______________________________ Relation to main subject: ___________________

Mother/Father of: ______________________________Child of: _______________________________

Ethnic Origin: ____

*For Ethnicity, please use "Irish, German, English", not "White" or use "Argentinian, Spanish, Brazilian", not "Hispanic". We will need to know where their roots are from.

Reason for Death: ____

Occupation/Trade: ________________________________ State/Country of death: _______________

~~~~~~

Was this person ever diagnosed with Cancer? _________

If so, at what age was the first diagnosis? _______

Type of Cancer:

BREAST   OVARIAN   COLON   PROSTATE   MELANOMA   ________________

LUNG   NON-HODGKIN LYMPHOMA   PANCREATIC   LEUKEMIA

What was the prognosis and treatment? Was treatment successful?

____

Was Genetic testing done and if so, were any mutations found that would indicate a higher chance of cancer? ____

Is there an occurrence of Ashkenazi Jewish ancestry? YES / NO

If yes, which family member does it originate from? ___________________
~~~~~~

Please check below if any of these conditions apply. For each check, please use the additional space for explanations. Things like age when diagnosed and severity are helpful.

♡ ARTHRITIS
♡ BIRTH DEFECTS
♡ HIGH CHOLESTROL
♡ MENTAL RETARDATION
♡ CLINICAL DEPRESSION
♡ MULTIPLE MISCARRIGAGES
♡ OBESITY
♡ OSTEOPOROSIS
♡ INFERTILITY
♡ EARLY/DELAYED PUBERTY
♡ SPECTRUM/AUTISM
♡ LUNG DISEASE
♡ KIDNEY DISEASE
♡ ALLERGIES TO MEDICATIONS

♡ HEARING LOSS
♡ HIGH BLOOD PRESSURE
♡ PHYSICAL ABNORMALITIES
♡ STROKE
♡ VISION LOSS
♡ ASTHMA
♡ DIABETES
♡ HEART DISEASE
♡ VERY TALL OR VERY SHORT STATURE
    *Compared to the rest of the family
♡ BIRTH MARKS
♡ BLOOD CLOTTING DISORDERS
♡ ALZHEIMER'S/DIMENTIA
♡ GOUT

NAME: ____

Date of Birth: _________ Date of Death: _________ State/country of birth: _______________________

Part of a multiple birth? YES / NO

Spouse: _______________________________ Relation to main subject: _____________________

Mother/Father of: _______________________________Child of: _______________________________

Ethnic Origin: ____

*For Ethnicity, please use "Irish, German, English", not "White" or use "Argentinian, Spanish, Brazilian", not "Hispanic". We will need to know where their roots are from.

Reason for Death: ____

Occupation/Trade: _______________________________ State/Country of death: _______________

~~~~~~

Was this person ever diagnosed with Cancer? _________

If so, at what age was the first diagnosis? _______

Type of Cancer:

BREAST   OVARIAN   COLON   PROSTATE   MELANOMA   _______________

LUNG   NON-HODGKIN LYMPHOMA   PANCREATIC   LEUKEMIA

What was the prognosis and treatment? Was treatment successful?

____

Was Genetic testing done and if so, were any mutations found that would indicate a higher chance of cancer? ____

Is there an occurrence of Ashkenazi Jewish ancestry? YES / NO

If yes, which family member does it originate from? ___________________________
~~~~~~

Please check below if any of these conditions apply. For each check, please use the additional space for explanations. Things like age when diagnosed and severity are helpful.

♡ ARTHRITIS	♡ HEARING LOSS
♡ BIRTH DEFECTS	♡ HIGH BLOOD PRESSURE
♡ HIGH CHOLESTROL	♡ PHYSICAL ABNORMALITIES
♡ MENTAL RETARDATION	♡ STROKE
♡ CLINICAL DEPRESSION	♡ VISION LOSS
♡ MULTIPLE MISCARRIGAGES	♡ ASTHMA
♡ OBESITY	♡ DIABETES
♡ OSTEOPOROSIS	♡ HEART DISEASE
♡ INFERTILITY	♡ VERY TALL OR VERY SHORT STATURE
♡ EARLY/DELAYED PUBERTY	*Compared to the rest of the family
♡ SPECTRUM/AUTISM	♡ BIRTH MARKS
♡ LUNG DISEASE	♡ BLOOD CLOTTING DISORDERS
♡ KIDNEY DISEASE	♡ ALZHEIMER'S/DIMENTIA
♡ ALLERGIES TO MEDICATIONS	♡ GOUT

NAME: ____

Date of Birth: _________   Date of Death: _________   State/country of birth: _________________

Part of a multiple birth? YES / NO

Spouse: _______________________   Relation to main subject: _________________

Mother/Father of: _______________________Child of: _______________________

Ethnic Origin: ____

*For Ethnicity, please use "Irish, German, English", not "White" or use "Argentinian, Spanish, Brazilian", not "Hispanic". We will need to know where their roots are from.

Reason for Death: ____

Occupation/Trade: _______________________   State/Country of death: _______________

~~~~~~

Was this person ever diagnosed with Cancer? _________

If so, at what age was the first diagnosis? _______

Type of Cancer:

BREAST   OVARIAN   COLON   PROSTATE   MELANOMA   _______________

LUNG   NON-HODGKIN LYMPHOMA   PANCREATIC   LEUKEMIA

What was the prognosis and treatment? Was treatment successful?

____

Was Genetic testing done and if so, were any mutations found that would indicate a higher chance of cancer? ____

Is there an occurrence of Ashkenazi Jewish ancestry? YES / NO

If yes, which family member does it originate from? _________________________
~~~~~~

Please check below if any of these conditions apply. For each check, please use the additional space for explanations. Things like age when diagnosed and severity are helpful.

♡ ARTHRITIS	♡ HEARING LOSS
♡ BIRTH DEFECTS	♡ HIGH BLOOD PRESSURE
♡ HIGH CHOLESTROL	♡ PHYSICAL ABNORMALITIES
♡ MENTAL RETARDATION	♡ STROKE
♡ CLINICAL DEPRESSION	♡ VISION LOSS
♡ MULTIPLE MISCARRIGAGES	♡ ASTHMA
♡ OBESITY	♡ DIABETES
♡ OSTEOPOROSIS	♡ HEART DISEASE
♡ INFERTILITY	♡ VERY TALL OR VERY SHORT STATURE
♡ EARLY/DELAYED PUBERTY	*Compared to the rest of the family
♡ SPECTRUM/AUTISM	♡ BIRTH MARKS
♡ LUNG DISEASE	♡ BLOOD CLOTTING DISORDERS
♡ KIDNEY DISEASE	♡ ALZHEIMER'S/DIMENTIA
♡ ALLERGIES TO MEDICATIONS	♡ GOUT

NAME: ____

Date of Birth: _________ Date of Death: _________ State/country of birth: ___________________

Part of a multiple birth? YES / NO

Spouse: _______________________________ Relation to main subject: ___________________

Mother/Father of: ______________________________Child of: _________________________________

Ethnic Origin: ____

*For Ethnicity, please use "Irish, German, English", not "White" or use "Argentinian, Spanish, Brazilian", not "Hispanic". We will need to know where their roots are from.

Reason for Death: ____

Occupation/Trade: _______________________________ State/Country of death: ________________

~~~~~~

Was this person ever diagnosed with Cancer? _________

If so, at what age was the first diagnosis? _______

Type of Cancer:

BREAST   OVARIAN   COLON   PROSTATE   MELANOMA   ________________

LUNG   NON-HODGKIN LYMPHOMA   PANCREATIC   LEUKEMIA

What was the prognosis and treatment? Was treatment successful?

____

Was Genetic testing done and if so, were any mutations found that would indicate a higher chance of cancer? ____

Is there an occurrence of Ashkenazi Jewish ancestry? YES / NO

If yes, which family member does it originate from? ___________________________
~~~~~~

Please check below if any of these conditions apply. For each check, please use the additional space for explanations. Things like age when diagnosed and severity are helpful.

- ♡ ARTHRITIS
- ♡ BIRTH DEFECTS
- ♡ HIGH CHOLESTROL
- ♡ MENTAL RETARDATION
- ♡ CLINICAL DEPRESSION
- ♡ MULTIPLE MISCARRIGAGES
- ♡ OBESITY
- ♡ OSTEOPOROSIS
- ♡ INFERTILITY
- ♡ EARLY/DELAYED PUBERTY
- ♡ SPECTRUM/AUTISM
- ♡ LUNG DISEASE
- ♡ KIDNEY DISEASE
- ♡ ALLERGIES TO MEDICATIONS

- ♡ HEARING LOSS
- ♡ HIGH BLOOD PRESSURE
- ♡ PHYSICAL ABNORMALITIES
- ♡ STROKE
- ♡ VISION LOSS
- ♡ ASTHMA
- ♡ DIABETES
- ♡ HEART DISEASE
- ♡ VERY TALL OR VERY SHORT STATURE
    *Compared to the rest of the family
- ♡ BIRTH MARKS
- ♡ BLOOD CLOTTING DISORDERS
- ♡ ALZHEIMER'S/DIMENTIA
- ♡ GOUT

NAME: ____

Date of Birth: _________   Date of Death: __________   State/country of birth: _________________

Part of a multiple birth? YES / NO

Spouse: ______________________________   Relation to main subject: _________________

Mother/Father of: _______________________Child of: _______________________________

Ethnic Origin: ____

*For Ethnicity, please use "Irish, German, English", not "White" or use "Argentinian, Spanish, Brazilian", not "Hispanic". We will need to know where their roots are from.

Reason for Death: ____

Occupation/Trade: ______________________________   State/Country of death: ____________

~~~~~~

Was this person ever diagnosed with Cancer? _________

If so, at what age was the first diagnosis? _______

Type of Cancer:

BREAST   OVARIAN   COLON   PROSTATE   MELANOMA   _______________

LUNG   NON-HODGKIN LYMPHOMA   PANCREATIC   LEUKEMIA

What was the prognosis and treatment? Was treatment successful?

____

Was Genetic testing done and if so, were any mutations found that would indicate a higher chance of cancer? ____

Is there an occurrence of Ashkenazi Jewish ancestry? YES / NO

If yes, which family member does it originate from? _____________________
~~~~~~

Please check below if any of these conditions apply. For each check, please use the additional space for explanations. Things like age when diagnosed and severity are helpful.

- ♡ ARTHRITIS
- ♡ BIRTH DEFECTS
- ♡ HIGH CHOLESTROL
- ♡ MENTAL RETARDATION
- ♡ CLINICAL DEPRESSION
- ♡ MULTIPLE MISCARRIGAGES
- ♡ OBESITY
- ♡ OSTEOPOROSIS
- ♡ INFERTILITY
- ♡ EARLY/DELAYED PUBERTY
- ♡ SPECTRUM/AUTISM
- ♡ LUNG DISEASE
- ♡ KIDNEY DISEASE
- ♡ ALLERGIES TO MEDICATIONS

- ♡ HEARING LOSS
- ♡ HIGH BLOOD PRESSURE
- ♡ PHYSICAL ABNORMALITIES
- ♡ STROKE
- ♡ VISION LOSS
- ♡ ASTHMA
- ♡ DIABETES
- ♡ HEART DISEASE
- ♡ VERY TALL OR VERY SHORT STATURE
      *Compared to the rest of the family
- ♡ BIRTH MARKS
- ♡ BLOOD CLOTTING DISORDERS
- ♡ ALZHEIMER'S/DIMENTIA
- ♡ GOUT

NAME: ____

Date of Birth: _________ Date of Death: _________ State/country of birth: _______________________

Part of a multiple birth? YES / NO

Spouse: _______________________________ Relation to main subject: ___________________________

Mother/Father of: _________________________________Child of: _______________________________

Ethnic Origin: ____

*For Ethnicity, please use "Irish, German, English", not "White" or use "Argentinian, Spanish, Brazilian", not "Hispanic". We will need to know where their roots are from.

Reason for Death: ____

Occupation/Trade: _______________________________ State/Country of death: _________________

~~~~~~

Was this person ever diagnosed with Cancer? _________

If so, at what age was the first diagnosis? _______

Type of Cancer:

BREAST   OVARIAN   COLON   PROSTATE   MELANOMA   _________________

LUNG   NON-HODGKIN LYMPHOMA   PANCREATIC   LEUKEMIA

What was the prognosis and treatment? Was treatment successful?

____

Was Genetic testing done and if so, were any mutations found that would indicate a higher chance of cancer? ____

Is there an occurrence of Ashkenazi Jewish ancestry? YES / NO

If yes, which family member does it originate from? _______________________________
~~~~~~

Please check below if any of these conditions apply. For each check, please use the additional space for explanations. Things like age when diagnosed and severity are helpful.

- ♡ ARTHRITIS
- ♡ BIRTH DEFECTS
- ♡ HIGH CHOLESTROL
- ♡ MENTAL RETARDATION
- ♡ CLINICAL DEPRESSION
- ♡ MULTIPLE MISCARRIGAGES
- ♡ OBESITY
- ♡ OSTEOPOROSIS
- ♡ INFERTILITY
- ♡ EARLY/DELAYED PUBERTY
- ♡ SPECTRUM/AUTISM
- ♡ LUNG DISEASE
- ♡ KIDNEY DISEASE
- ♡ ALLERGIES TO MEDICATIONS

- ♡ HEARING LOSS
- ♡ HIGH BLOOD PRESSURE
- ♡ PHYSICAL ABNORMALITIES
- ♡ STROKE
- ♡ VISION LOSS
- ♡ ASTHMA
- ♡ DIABETES
- ♡ HEART DISEASE
- ♡ VERY TALL OR VERY SHORT STATURE
     *Compared to the rest of the family
- ♡ BIRTH MARKS
- ♡ BLOOD CLOTTING DISORDERS
- ♡ ALZHEIMER'S/DIMENTIA
- ♡ GOUT

NAME: ____

Date of Birth: _________ Date of Death: _________ State/country of birth: _______________

Part of a multiple birth? YES / NO

Spouse: _______________________________ Relation to main subject: _______________________

Mother/Father of: _______________________Child of: _______________________________

Ethnic Origin: ____

*For Ethnicity, please use "Irish, German, English", not "White" or use "Argentinian, Spanish, Brazilian", not "Hispanic". We will need to know where their roots are from.

Reason for Death: ____

Occupation/Trade: ______________________________ State/Country of death: ______________

~~~~~~

Was this person ever diagnosed with Cancer? _________

If so, at what age was the first diagnosis? _______

Type of Cancer:

BREAST   OVARIAN   COLON   PROSTATE   MELANOMA   _______________

LUNG   NON-HODGKIN LYMPHOMA   PANCREATIC   LEUKEMIA

What was the prognosis and treatment? Was treatment successful?

____

Was Genetic testing done and if so, were any mutations found that would indicate a higher chance of cancer? ____

Is there an occurrence of Ashkenazi Jewish ancestry? YES / NO

If yes, which family member does it originate from? ___________________
~~~~~~

Please check below if any of these conditions apply. For each check, please use the additional space for explanations. Things like age when diagnosed and severity are helpful.

♡ ARTHRITIS		♡ HEARING LOSS	
♡ BIRTH DEFECTS		♡ HIGH BLOOD PRESSURE	
♡ HIGH CHOLESTROL		♡ PHYSICAL ABNORMALITIES	
♡ MENTAL RETARDATION		♡ STROKE	
♡ CLINICAL DEPRESSION		♡ VISION LOSS	
♡ MULTIPLE MISCARRIGAGES		♡ ASTHMA	
♡ OBESITY		♡ DIABETES	
♡ OSTEOPOROSIS		♡ HEART DISEASE	
♡ INFERTILITY		♡ VERY TALL OR VERY SHORT STATURE	
♡ EARLY/DELAYED PUBERTY		*Compared to the rest of the family	
♡ SPECTRUM/AUTISM		♡ BIRTH MARKS	
♡ LUNG DISEASE		♡ BLOOD CLOTTING DISORDERS	
♡ KIDNEY DISEASE		♡ ALZHEIMER'S/DIMENTIA	
♡ ALLERGIES TO MEDICATIONS		♡ GOUT	

NAME: ____

Date of Birth: _________ Date of Death: _________ State/country of birth: _________________

Part of a multiple birth? YES / NO

Spouse: _______________________________ Relation to main subject: _________________

Mother/Father of: _______________________________Child of: _______________________________

Ethnic Origin: ____

*For Ethnicity, please use "Irish, German, English", not "White" or use "Argentinian, Spanish, Brazilian", not "Hispanic". We will need to know where their roots are from.

Reason for Death: ____

Occupation/Trade: _______________________________ State/Country of death: _______________

~~~~~~

Was this person ever diagnosed with Cancer? _________

If so, at what age was the first diagnosis? _______

Type of Cancer:

BREAST   OVARIAN   COLON   PROSTATE   MELANOMA   _________________

LUNG   NON-HODGKIN LYMPHOMA   PANCREATIC   LEUKEMIA

What was the prognosis and treatment? Was treatment successful?

____

Was Genetic testing done and if so, were any mutations found that would indicate a higher chance of cancer? ____

Is there an occurrence of Ashkenazi Jewish ancestry? YES / NO

If yes, which family member does it originate from? _____________________
~~~~~~

Please check below if any of these conditions apply. For each check, please use the additional space for explanations. Things like age when diagnosed and severity are helpful.

- ♡ ARTHRITIS
- ♡ BIRTH DEFECTS
- ♡ HIGH CHOLESTROL
- ♡ MENTAL RETARDATION
- ♡ CLINICAL DEPRESSION
- ♡ MULTIPLE MISCARRIGAGES
- ♡ OBESITY
- ♡ OSTEOPOROSIS
- ♡ INFERTILITY
- ♡ EARLY/DELAYED PUBERTY
- ♡ SPECTRUM/AUTISM
- ♡ LUNG DISEASE
- ♡ KIDNEY DISEASE
- ♡ ALLERGIES TO MEDICATIONS

- ♡ HEARING LOSS
- ♡ HIGH BLOOD PRESSURE
- ♡ PHYSICAL ABNORMALITIES
- ♡ STROKE
- ♡ VISION LOSS
- ♡ ASTHMA
- ♡ DIABETES
- ♡ HEART DISEASE
- ♡ VERY TALL OR VERY SHORT STATURE
    *Compared to the rest of the family
- ♡ BIRTH MARKS
- ♡ BLOOD CLOTTING DISORDERS
- ♡ ALZHEIMER'S/DIMENTIA
- ♡ GOUT

NAME: ____

Date of Birth: _________ Date of Death: _________ State/country of birth: __________________

Part of a multiple birth? YES / NO

Spouse: _______________________________ Relation to main subject: ___________________

Mother/Father of: _________________________________Child of: ______________________________

Ethnic Origin: ____

*For Ethnicity, please use "Irish, German, English", not "White" or use "Argentinian, Spanish, Brazilian", not "Hispanic". We will need to know where their roots are from.

Reason for Death: ____

Occupation/Trade: _____________________________________ State/Country of death: ______________

~~~~~~

Was this person ever diagnosed with Cancer? _________

If so, at what age was the first diagnosis? _______

Type of Cancer:

BREAST   OVARIAN   COLON   PROSTATE   MELANOMA   ____________________

LUNG   NON-HODGKIN LYMPHOMA   PANCREATIC   LEUKEMIA

What was the prognosis and treatment? Was treatment successful?

____

Was Genetic testing done and if so, were any mutations found that would indicate a higher chance of cancer? ____

Is there an occurrence of Ashkenazi Jewish ancestry? YES / NO

If yes, which family member does it originate from? ____________________________
~~~~~~

Please check below if any of these conditions apply. For each check, please use the additional space for explanations. Things like age when diagnosed and severity are helpful.

- ♡ ARTHRITIS
- ♡ BIRTH DEFECTS
- ♡ HIGH CHOLESTROL
- ♡ MENTAL RETARDATION
- ♡ CLINICAL DEPRESSION
- ♡ MULTIPLE MISCARRIGAGES
- ♡ OBESITY
- ♡ OSTEOPOROSIS
- ♡ INFERTILITY
- ♡ EARLY/DELAYED PUBERTY
- ♡ SPECTRUM/AUTISM
- ♡ LUNG DISEASE
- ♡ KIDNEY DISEASE
- ♡ ALLERGIES TO MEDICATIONS

- ♡ HEARING LOSS
- ♡ HIGH BLOOD PRESSURE
- ♡ PHYSICAL ABNORMALITIES
- ♡ STROKE
- ♡ VISION LOSS
- ♡ ASTHMA
- ♡ DIABETES
- ♡ HEART DISEASE
- ♡ VERY TALL OR VERY SHORT STATURE
  - *Compared to the rest of the family
- ♡ BIRTH MARKS
- ♡ BLOOD CLOTTING DISORDERS
- ♡ ALZHEIMER'S/DIMENTIA
- ♡ GOUT

NAME: ____

Date of Birth: _________ Date of Death: _________ State/country of birth: _______________

Part of a multiple birth? YES / NO

Spouse: _______________________________ Relation to main subject: ___________________

Mother/Father of: _______________________________Child of: ___________________________

Ethnic Origin: ____

*For Ethnicity, please use "Irish, German, English", not "White" or use "Argentinian, Spanish, Brazilian", not "Hispanic". We will need to know where their roots are from.

Reason for Death: ____

Occupation/Trade: _______________________________ State/Country of death: _____________

~~~~~~

Was this person ever diagnosed with Cancer? _________

If so, at what age was the first diagnosis? _______

Type of Cancer:

BREAST   OVARIAN   COLON   PROSTATE   MELANOMA   ________________

LUNG   NON-HODGKIN LYMPHOMA   PANCREATIC   LEUKEMIA

What was the prognosis and treatment? Was treatment successful?

____

Was Genetic testing done and if so, were any mutations found that would indicate a higher chance of cancer? ____

Is there an occurrence of Ashkenazi Jewish ancestry? YES / NO

If yes, which family member does it originate from? _____________________
~~~~~~

Please check below if any of these conditions apply. For each check, please use the additional space for explanations. Things like age when diagnosed and severity are helpful.

♡ ARTHRITIS
♡ BIRTH DEFECTS
♡ HIGH CHOLESTROL
♡ MENTAL RETARDATION
♡ CLINICAL DEPRESSION
♡ MULTIPLE MISCARRIGAGES
♡ OBESITY
♡ OSTEOPOROSIS
♡ INFERTILITY
♡ EARLY/DELAYED PUBERTY
♡ SPECTRUM/AUTISM
♡ LUNG DISEASE
♡ KIDNEY DISEASE
♡ ALLERGIES TO MEDICATIONS

♡ HEARING LOSS
♡ HIGH BLOOD PRESSURE
♡ PHYSICAL ABNORMALITIES
♡ STROKE
♡ VISION LOSS
♡ ASTHMA
♡ DIABETES
♡ HEART DISEASE
♡ VERY TALL OR VERY SHORT STATURE
     *Compared to the rest of the family
♡ BIRTH MARKS
♡ BLOOD CLOTTING DISORDERS
♡ ALZHEIMER'S/DIMENTIA
♡ GOUT

NAME: ____

Date of Birth: _________ Date of Death: _________ State/country of birth: _______________

Part of a multiple birth? YES / NO

Spouse: _______________________________ Relation to main subject: _______________________

Mother/Father of: _______________________________Child of: _______________________________

Ethnic Origin: ____

*For Ethnicity, please use "Irish, German, English", not "White" or use "Argentinian, Spanish, Brazilian", not "Hispanic". We will need to know where their roots are from.

Reason for Death: ____

Occupation/Trade: _______________________________ State/Country of death: _______________

~~~~~~

Was this person ever diagnosed with Cancer? _________

If so, at what age was the first diagnosis? _______

Type of Cancer:

BREAST   OVARIAN   COLON   PROSTATE   MELANOMA   ________________

LUNG   NON-HODGKIN LYMPHOMA   PANCREATIC   LEUKEMIA

What was the prognosis and treatment? Was treatment successful?

____

Was Genetic testing done and if so, were any mutations found that would indicate a higher chance of cancer? ____

Is there an occurrence of Ashkenazi Jewish ancestry? YES / NO

If yes, which family member does it originate from? ___________________________
~~~~~~

Please check below if any of these conditions apply. For each check, please use the additional space for explanations. Things like age when diagnosed and severity are helpful.

♡ ARTHRITIS
♡ BIRTH DEFECTS
♡ HIGH CHOLESTROL
♡ MENTAL RETARDATION
♡ CLINICAL DEPRESSION
♡ MULTIPLE MISCARRIGAGES
♡ OBESITY
♡ OSTEOPOROSIS
♡ INFERTILITY
♡ EARLY/DELAYED PUBERTY
♡ SPECTRUM/AUTISM
♡ LUNG DISEASE
♡ KIDNEY DISEASE
♡ ALLERGIES TO MEDICATIONS

♡ HEARING LOSS
♡ HIGH BLOOD PRESSURE
♡ PHYSICAL ABNORMALITIES
♡ STROKE
♡ VISION LOSS
♡ ASTHMA
♡ DIABETES
♡ HEART DISEASE
♡ VERY TALL OR VERY SHORT STATURE
　　*Compared to the rest of the family
♡ BIRTH MARKS
♡ BLOOD CLOTTING DISORDERS
♡ ALZHEIMER'S/DIMENTIA
♡ GOUT

NAME: ____

Date of Birth: _________ Date of Death: _________ State/country of birth: ________________

Part of a multiple birth? YES / NO

Spouse: _______________________________ Relation to main subject: ___________________

Mother/Father of: ______________________________Child of: ______________________________

Ethnic Origin: ____

*For Ethnicity, please use "Irish, German, English", not "White" or use "Argentinian, Spanish, Brazilian", not "Hispanic". We will need to know where their roots are from.

Reason for Death: ____

Occupation/Trade: _______________________________ State/Country of death: _____________

~~~~~~

Was this person ever diagnosed with Cancer? _________

If so, at what age was the first diagnosis? _______

Type of Cancer:

BREAST   OVARIAN   COLON   PROSTATE   MELANOMA   ________________

LUNG   NON-HODGKIN LYMPHOMA   PANCREATIC   LEUKEMIA

What was the prognosis and treatment? Was treatment successful?

____

Was Genetic testing done and if so, were any mutations found that would indicate a higher chance of cancer? ____

Is there an occurrence of Ashkenazi Jewish ancestry? YES / NO

If yes, which family member does it originate from? ___________________________
~~~~~~

Please check below if any of these conditions apply. For each check, please use the additional space for explanations. Things like age when diagnosed and severity are helpful.

♡ ARTHRITIS
♡ BIRTH DEFECTS
♡ HIGH CHOLESTROL
♡ MENTAL RETARDATION
♡ CLINICAL DEPRESSION
♡ MULTIPLE MISCARRIGAGES
♡ OBESITY
♡ OSTEOPOROSIS
♡ INFERTILITY
♡ EARLY/DELAYED PUBERTY
♡ SPECTRUM/AUTISM
♡ LUNG DISEASE
♡ KIDNEY DISEASE
♡ ALLERGIES TO MEDICATIONS

♡ HEARING LOSS
♡ HIGH BLOOD PRESSURE
♡ PHYSICAL ABNORMALITIES
♡ STROKE
♡ VISION LOSS
♡ ASTHMA
♡ DIABETES
♡ HEART DISEASE
♡ VERY TALL OR VERY SHORT STATURE
    *Compared to the rest of the family
♡ BIRTH MARKS
♡ BLOOD CLOTTING DISORDERS
♡ ALZHEIMER'S/DIMENTIA
♡ GOUT

NAME: ____

Date of Birth: _________ Date of Death: _________ State/country of birth: _________________

Part of a multiple birth? YES / NO

Spouse: _______________________________ Relation to main subject: _________________

Mother/Father of: _______________________________Child of: _________________________

Ethnic Origin: ____

*For Ethnicity, please use "Irish, German, English", not "White" or use "Argentinian, Spanish, Brazilian", not "Hispanic". We will need to know where their roots are from.

Reason for Death: ____

Occupation/Trade: _______________________________ State/Country of death: _______________

~~~~~~

Was this person ever diagnosed with Cancer? _________

If so, at what age was the first diagnosis? _______

Type of Cancer:

BREAST   OVARIAN   COLON   PROSTATE   MELANOMA   _______________

LUNG   NON-HODGKIN LYMPHOMA   PANCREATIC   LEUKEMIA

What was the prognosis and treatment? Was treatment successful?

____

Was Genetic testing done and if so, were any mutations found that would indicate a higher chance of cancer? ____

Is there an occurrence of Ashkenazi Jewish ancestry? YES / NO

If yes, which family member does it originate from? ___________________________
~~~~~~

Please check below if any of these conditions apply. For each check, please use the additional space for explanations. Things like age when diagnosed and severity are helpful.

♡ ARTHRITIS
♡ BIRTH DEFECTS
♡ HIGH CHOLESTROL
♡ MENTAL RETARDATION
♡ CLINICAL DEPRESSION
♡ MULTIPLE MISCARRIGAGES
♡ OBESITY
♡ OSTEOPOROSIS
♡ INFERTILITY
♡ EARLY/DELAYED PUBERTY
♡ SPECTRUM/AUTISM
♡ LUNG DISEASE
♡ KIDNEY DISEASE
♡ ALLERGIES TO MEDICATIONS

♡ HEARING LOSS
♡ HIGH BLOOD PRESSURE
♡ PHYSICAL ABNORMALITIES
♡ STROKE
♡ VISION LOSS
♡ ASTHMA
♡ DIABETES
♡ HEART DISEASE
♡ VERY TALL OR VERY SHORT STATURE
    *Compared to the rest of the family
♡ BIRTH MARKS
♡ BLOOD CLOTTING DISORDERS
♡ ALZHEIMER'S/DIMENTIA
♡ GOUT

NAME: ____

Date of Birth: __________ Date of Death: __________ State/country of birth: _________________

Part of a multiple birth? YES / NO

Spouse: _______________________________ Relation to main subject: __________________

Mother/Father of: _______________________Child of: ______________________________

Ethnic Origin: ____

*For Ethnicity, please use "Irish, German, English", not "White" or use "Argentinian, Spanish, Brazilian", not "Hispanic". We will need to know where their roots are from.

Reason for Death: ____

Occupation/Trade: _______________________________ State/Country of death: _______________

~~~~~~

Was this person ever diagnosed with Cancer? __________

If so, at what age was the first diagnosis? _______

Type of Cancer:

BREAST   OVARIAN   COLON   PROSTATE   MELANOMA   ____________________

LUNG   NON-HODGKIN LYMPHOMA   PANCREATIC   LEUKEMIA

What was the prognosis and treatment? Was treatment successful?

____

Was Genetic testing done and if so, were any mutations found that would indicate a higher chance of cancer? ____

Is there an occurrence of Ashkenazi Jewish ancestry? YES / NO

If yes, which family member does it originate from? ___________________________
~~~~~~

Please check below if any of these conditions apply. For each check, please use the additional space for explanations. Things like age when diagnosed and severity are helpful.

- ♡ ARTHRITIS
- ♡ BIRTH DEFECTS
- ♡ HIGH CHOLESTROL
- ♡ MENTAL RETARDATION
- ♡ CLINICAL DEPRESSION
- ♡ MULTIPLE MISCARRIGAGES
- ♡ OBESITY
- ♡ OSTEOPOROSIS
- ♡ INFERTILITY
- ♡ EARLY/DELAYED PUBERTY
- ♡ SPECTRUM/AUTISM
- ♡ LUNG DISEASE
- ♡ KIDNEY DISEASE
- ♡ ALLERGIES TO MEDICATIONS

- ♡ HEARING LOSS
- ♡ HIGH BLOOD PRESSURE
- ♡ PHYSICAL ABNORMALITIES
- ♡ STROKE
- ♡ VISION LOSS
- ♡ ASTHMA
- ♡ DIABETES
- ♡ HEART DISEASE
- ♡ VERY TALL OR VERY SHORT STATURE
    *Compared to the rest of the family
- ♡ BIRTH MARKS
- ♡ BLOOD CLOTTING DISORDERS
- ♡ ALZHEIMER'S/DIMENTIA
- ♡ GOUT

NAME: ____

Date of Birth: _________   Date of Death: _________ State/country of birth: _________________

Part of a multiple birth? YES / NO

Spouse: _________________________________   Relation to main subject: ___________________

Mother/Father of: _______________________________Child of: _________________________________

Ethnic Origin: ____

*For Ethnicity, please use "Irish, German, English", not "White" or use "Argentinian, Spanish, Brazilian", not "Hispanic". We will need to know where their roots are from.

Reason for Death: ____

Occupation/Trade: _______________________________   State/Country of death: _______________

~~~~~~

Was this person ever diagnosed with Cancer? _________

If so, at what age was the first diagnosis? _______

Type of Cancer:

BREAST   OVARIAN   COLON   PROSTATE   MELANOMA   ________________

LUNG   NON-HODGKIN LYMPHOMA   PANCREATIC   LEUKEMIA

What was the prognosis and treatment? Was treatment successful?

____

Was Genetic testing done and if so, were any mutations found that would indicate a higher chance of cancer? ____

Is there an occurrence of Ashkenazi Jewish ancestry? YES / NO

If yes, which family member does it originate from? ___________________________
~~~~~~

Please check below if any of these conditions apply. For each check, please use the additional space for explanations. Things like age when diagnosed and severity are helpful.

♡ ARTHRITIS	♡ HEARING LOSS
♡ BIRTH DEFECTS	♡ HIGH BLOOD PRESSURE
♡ HIGH CHOLESTROL	♡ PHYSICAL ABNORMALITIES
♡ MENTAL RETARDATION	♡ STROKE
♡ CLINICAL DEPRESSION	♡ VISION LOSS
♡ MULTIPLE MISCARRIGAGES	♡ ASTHMA
♡ OBESITY	♡ DIABETES
♡ OSTEOPOROSIS	♡ HEART DISEASE
♡ INFERTILITY	♡ VERY TALL OR VERY SHORT STATURE
♡ EARLY/DELAYED PUBERTY	*Compared to the rest of the family
♡ SPECTRUM/AUTISM	♡ BIRTH MARKS
♡ LUNG DISEASE	♡ BLOOD CLOTTING DISORDERS
♡ KIDNEY DISEASE	♡ ALZHEIMER'S/DIMENTIA
♡ ALLERGIES TO MEDICATIONS	♡ GOUT

NAME: ____

Date of Birth: _________ Date of Death: _________ State/country of birth: ________________

Part of a multiple birth? YES / NO

Spouse: ______________________________ Relation to main subject: ________________

Mother/Father of: _______________________________Child of: _________________________________

Ethnic Origin: ____

*For Ethnicity, please use "Irish, German, English", not "White" or use "Argentinian, Spanish, Brazilian", not "Hispanic". We will need to know where their roots are from.

Reason for Death: ____

Occupation/Trade: ______________________________ State/Country of death: ______________

~~~~~~

Was this person ever diagnosed with Cancer? _________

If so, at what age was the first diagnosis? _______

Type of Cancer:

BREAST   OVARIAN   COLON   PROSTATE   MELANOMA   ________________

LUNG   NON-HODGKIN LYMPHOMA   PANCREATIC   LEUKEMIA

What was the prognosis and treatment? Was treatment successful?

____

Was Genetic testing done and if so, were any mutations found that would indicate a higher chance of cancer? ____

Is there an occurrence of Ashkenazi Jewish ancestry? YES / NO

If yes, which family member does it originate from? ____________________________
~~~~~~

Please check below if any of these conditions apply. For each check, please use the additional space for explanations. Things like age when diagnosed and severity are helpful.

♡ ARTHRITIS
♡ BIRTH DEFECTS
♡ HIGH CHOLESTROL
♡ MENTAL RETARDATION
♡ CLINICAL DEPRESSION
♡ MULTIPLE MISCARRIGAGES
♡ OBESITY
♡ OSTEOPOROSIS
♡ INFERTILITY
♡ EARLY/DELAYED PUBERTY
♡ SPECTRUM/AUTISM
♡ LUNG DISEASE
♡ KIDNEY DISEASE
♡ ALLERGIES TO MEDICATIONS

♡ HEARING LOSS
♡ HIGH BLOOD PRESSURE
♡ PHYSICAL ABNORMALITIES
♡ STROKE
♡ VISION LOSS
♡ ASTHMA
♡ DIABETES
♡ HEART DISEASE
♡ VERY TALL OR VERY SHORT STATURE
     *Compared to the rest of the family
♡ BIRTH MARKS
♡ BLOOD CLOTTING DISORDERS
♡ ALZHEIMER'S/DIMENTIA
♡ GOUT

NAME: ____

Date of Birth: _________   Date of Death: _________   State/country of birth: ________________

Part of a multiple birth? YES / NO

Spouse: ______________________________   Relation to main subject: ________________

Mother/Father of: ______________________________Child of: ________________________

Ethnic Origin: ____

*For Ethnicity, please use "Irish, German, English", not "White" or use "Argentinian, Spanish, Brazilian", not "Hispanic". We will need to know where their roots are from.

Reason for Death: ____

Occupation/Trade: ______________________________   State/Country of death: ______________

~~~~~~

Was this person ever diagnosed with Cancer? _________

If so, at what age was the first diagnosis? _______

Type of Cancer:

BREAST   OVARIAN   COLON   PROSTATE   MELANOMA   ________________

LUNG   NON-HODGKIN LYMPHOMA   PANCREATIC   LEUKEMIA

What was the prognosis and treatment? Was treatment successful?

____

Was Genetic testing done and if so, were any mutations found that would indicate a higher chance of cancer? ____

Is there an occurrence of Ashkenazi Jewish ancestry? YES / NO

If yes, which family member does it originate from? ____________________
~~~~~~

Please check below if any of these conditions apply. For each check, please use the additional space for explanations. Things like age when diagnosed and severity are helpful.

♡ ARTHRITIS
♡ BIRTH DEFECTS
♡ HIGH CHOLESTROL
♡ MENTAL RETARDATION
♡ CLINICAL DEPRESSION
♡ MULTIPLE MISCARRIGAGES
♡ OBESITY
♡ OSTEOPOROSIS
♡ INFERTILITY
♡ EARLY/DELAYED PUBERTY
♡ SPECTRUM/AUTISM
♡ LUNG DISEASE
♡ KIDNEY DISEASE
♡ ALLERGIES TO MEDICATIONS

♡ HEARING LOSS
♡ HIGH BLOOD PRESSURE
♡ PHYSICAL ABNORMALITIES
♡ STROKE
♡ VISION LOSS
♡ ASTHMA
♡ DIABETES
♡ HEART DISEASE
♡ VERY TALL OR VERY SHORT STATURE
        *Compared to the rest of the family
♡ BIRTH MARKS
♡ BLOOD CLOTTING DISORDERS
♡ ALZHEIMER'S/DIMENTIA
♡ GOUT

NAME: ____

Date of Birth: _________ Date of Death: _________ State/country of birth: _________________

Part of a multiple birth? YES / NO

Spouse: _______________________________ Relation to main subject: ___________________

Mother/Father of: _______________________________Child of: _________________________

Ethnic Origin: ____

*For Ethnicity, please use "Irish, German, English", not "White" or use "Argentinian, Spanish, Brazilian", not "Hispanic". We will need to know where their roots are from.

Reason for Death: ____

Occupation/Trade: _______________________________ State/Country of death: _____________

~~~~~~

Was this person ever diagnosed with Cancer? _________

If so, at what age was the first diagnosis? _______

Type of Cancer:

BREAST   OVARIAN   COLON   PROSTATE   MELANOMA   ________________

LUNG   NON-HODGKIN LYMPHOMA   PANCREATIC   LEUKEMIA

What was the prognosis and treatment? Was treatment successful?

____

Was Genetic testing done and if so, were any mutations found that would indicate a higher chance of cancer? ____

Is there an occurrence of Ashkenazi Jewish ancestry? YES / NO

If yes, which family member does it originate from? _____________________
~~~~~~

Please check below if any of these conditions apply. For each check, please use the additional space for explanations. Things like age when diagnosed and severity are helpful.

♡ ARTHRITIS
♡ BIRTH DEFECTS
♡ HIGH CHOLESTROL
♡ MENTAL RETARDATION
♡ CLINICAL DEPRESSION
♡ MULTIPLE MISCARRIGAGES
♡ OBESITY
♡ OSTEOPOROSIS
♡ INFERTILITY
♡ EARLY/DELAYED PUBERTY
♡ SPECTRUM/AUTISM
♡ LUNG DISEASE
♡ KIDNEY DISEASE
♡ ALLERGIES TO MEDICATIONS

♡ HEARING LOSS
♡ HIGH BLOOD PRESSURE
♡ PHYSICAL ABNORMALITIES
♡ STROKE
♡ VISION LOSS
♡ ASTHMA
♡ DIABETES
♡ HEART DISEASE
♡ VERY TALL OR VERY SHORT STATURE
     *Compared to the rest of the family
♡ BIRTH MARKS
♡ BLOOD CLOTTING DISORDERS
♡ ALZHEIMER'S/DIMENTIA
♡ GOUT

NAME: _______________________________________

Date of Birth: _________ Date of Death: _________ State/country of birth: _______________

Part of a multiple birth? YES / NO

Spouse: _______________________________ Relation to main subject: _______________________

Mother/Father of: _______________________________Child of: _______________________________

Ethnic Origin: ____

*For Ethnicity, please use "Irish, German, English", not "White" or use "Argentinian, Spanish, Brazilian", not "Hispanic". We will need to know where their roots are from.

Reason for Death: ____

Occupation/Trade: _______________________________ State/Country of death: _______________

~~~~~~

Was this person ever diagnosed with Cancer? _________

If so, at what age was the first diagnosis? _______

Type of Cancer:

BREAST   OVARIAN   COLON   PROSTATE   MELANOMA   _______________

LUNG   NON-HODGKIN LYMPHOMA   PANCREATIC   LEUKEMIA

What was the prognosis and treatment? Was treatment successful?

____

Was Genetic testing done and if so, were any mutations found that would indicate a higher chance of cancer? ____

Is there an occurrence of Ashkenazi Jewish ancestry? YES / NO

If yes, which family member does it originate from? _______________________
~~~~~~

Please check below if any of these conditions apply. For each check, please use the additional space for explanations. Things like age when diagnosed and severity are helpful.

♡ ARTHRITIS
♡ BIRTH DEFECTS
♡ HIGH CHOLESTROL
♡ MENTAL RETARDATION
♡ CLINICAL DEPRESSION
♡ MULTIPLE MISCARRIGAGES
♡ OBESITY
♡ OSTEOPOROSIS
♡ INFERTILITY
♡ EARLY/DELAYED PUBERTY
♡ SPECTRUM/AUTISM
♡ LUNG DISEASE
♡ KIDNEY DISEASE
♡ ALLERGIES TO MEDICATIONS

♡ HEARING LOSS
♡ HIGH BLOOD PRESSURE
♡ PHYSICAL ABNORMALITIES
♡ STROKE
♡ VISION LOSS
♡ ASTHMA
♡ DIABETES
♡ HEART DISEASE
♡ VERY TALL OR VERY SHORT STATURE
    *Compared to the rest of the family
♡ BIRTH MARKS
♡ BLOOD CLOTTING DISORDERS
♡ ALZHEIMER'S/DIMENTIA
♡ GOUT

NAME: ____

Date of Birth: __________ Date of Death: __________ State/country of birth: ___________________

Part of a multiple birth? YES / NO

Spouse: _______________________________ Relation to main subject: ___________________

Mother/Father of: ______________________________Child of: ___________________________

Ethnic Origin: ____

*For Ethnicity, please use "Irish, German, English", not "White" or use "Argentinian, Spanish, Brazilian", not "Hispanic". We will need to know where their roots are from.

Reason for Death: ____

Occupation/Trade: _______________________________ State/Country of death: ____________

~~~~~~

Was this person ever diagnosed with Cancer? __________

If so, at what age was the first diagnosis? _______

Type of Cancer:

BREAST   OVARIAN   COLON   PROSTATE   MELANOMA   ___________________

LUNG   NON-HODGKIN LYMPHOMA   PANCREATIC   LEUKEMIA

What was the prognosis and treatment? Was treatment successful?

____

Was Genetic testing done and if so, were any mutations found that would indicate a higher chance of cancer? ____

Is there an occurrence of Ashkenazi Jewish ancestry? YES / NO

If yes, which family member does it originate from? ___________________________
~~~~~~

Please check below if any of these conditions apply. For each check, please use the additional space for explanations. Things like age when diagnosed and severity are helpful.

- ♡ ARTHRITIS
- ♡ BIRTH DEFECTS
- ♡ HIGH CHOLESTROL
- ♡ MENTAL RETARDATION
- ♡ CLINICAL DEPRESSION
- ♡ MULTIPLE MISCARRIGAGES
- ♡ OBESITY
- ♡ OSTEOPOROSIS
- ♡ INFERTILITY
- ♡ EARLY/DELAYED PUBERTY
- ♡ SPECTRUM/AUTISM
- ♡ LUNG DISEASE
- ♡ KIDNEY DISEASE
- ♡ ALLERGIES TO MEDICATIONS

- ♡ HEARING LOSS
- ♡ HIGH BLOOD PRESSURE
- ♡ PHYSICAL ABNORMALITIES
- ♡ STROKE
- ♡ VISION LOSS
- ♡ ASTHMA
- ♡ DIABETES
- ♡ HEART DISEASE
- ♡ VERY TALL OR VERY SHORT STATURE
    *Compared to the rest of the family
- ♡ BIRTH MARKS
- ♡ BLOOD CLOTTING DISORDERS
- ♡ ALZHEIMER'S/DIMENTIA
- ♡ GOUT

NAME: _______________________________________

Date of Birth: _________ Date of Death: _________ State/country of birth: ___________________

Part of a multiple birth? YES / NO

Spouse: _______________________________ Relation to main subject: ___________________

Mother/Father of: _______________________________Child of: _______________________________

Ethnic Origin: ____

*For Ethnicity, please use "Irish, German, English", not "White" or use "Argentinian, Spanish, Brazilian", not "Hispanic". We will need to know where their roots are from.

Reason for Death: ____

Occupation/Trade: _______________________________ State/Country of death: _______________

~~~~~~

Was this person ever diagnosed with Cancer? _________

If so, at what age was the first diagnosis? _______

Type of Cancer:

BREAST   OVARIAN   COLON   PROSTATE   MELANOMA   _______________

LUNG   NON-HODGKIN LYMPHOMA   PANCREATIC   LEUKEMIA

What was the prognosis and treatment? Was treatment successful?

____

Was Genetic testing done and if so, were any mutations found that would indicate a higher chance of cancer? ____

Is there an occurrence of Ashkenazi Jewish ancestry? YES / NO

If yes, which family member does it originate from? ___________________
~~~~~~

Please check below if any of these conditions apply. For each check, please use the additional space for explanations. Things like age when diagnosed and severity are helpful.

♡ ARTHRITIS
♡ BIRTH DEFECTS
♡ HIGH CHOLESTROL
♡ MENTAL RETARDATION
♡ CLINICAL DEPRESSION
♡ MULTIPLE MISCARRIGAGES
♡ OBESITY
♡ OSTEOPOROSIS
♡ INFERTILITY
♡ EARLY/DELAYED PUBERTY
♡ SPECTRUM/AUTISM
♡ LUNG DISEASE
♡ KIDNEY DISEASE
♡ ALLERGIES TO MEDICATIONS

♡ HEARING LOSS
♡ HIGH BLOOD PRESSURE
♡ PHYSICAL ABNORMALITIES
♡ STROKE
♡ VISION LOSS
♡ ASTHMA
♡ DIABETES
♡ HEART DISEASE
♡ VERY TALL OR VERY SHORT STATURE
    *Compared to the rest of the family
♡ BIRTH MARKS
♡ BLOOD CLOTTING DISORDERS
♡ ALZHEIMER'S/DIMENTIA
♡ GOUT

NAME: ____

Date of Birth: _________   Date of Death: _________ State/country of birth: ____________________

Part of a multiple birth? YES / NO

Spouse: _______________________________   Relation to main subject: ___________________

Mother/Father of: ________________________________Child of: _______________________________

Ethnic Origin: ____

*For Ethnicity, please use "Irish, German, English", not "White" or use "Argentinian, Spanish, Brazilian", not "Hispanic". We will need to know where their roots are from.

Reason for Death: ____

Occupation/Trade: _________________________________   State/Country of death: ________________

~~~~~~

Was this person ever diagnosed with Cancer? __________

If so, at what age was the first diagnosis? _______

Type of Cancer:

BREAST   OVARIAN   COLON   PROSTATE   MELANOMA   ________________

LUNG   NON-HODGKIN LYMPHOMA   PANCREATIC   LEUKEMIA

What was the prognosis and treatment? Was treatment successful?

____

Was Genetic testing done and if so, were any mutations found that would indicate a higher chance of cancer? ____

Is there an occurrence of Ashkenazi Jewish ancestry? YES / NO

If yes, which family member does it originate from? _____________________________
~~~~~~

Please check below if any of these conditions apply. For each check, please use the additional space for explanations. Things like age when diagnosed and severity are helpful.

- ♡ ARTHRITIS
- ♡ BIRTH DEFECTS
- ♡ HIGH CHOLESTROL
- ♡ MENTAL RETARDATION
- ♡ CLINICAL DEPRESSION
- ♡ MULTIPLE MISCARRIGAGES
- ♡ OBESITY
- ♡ OSTEOPOROSIS
- ♡ INFERTILITY
- ♡ EARLY/DELAYED PUBERTY
- ♡ SPECTRUM/AUTISM
- ♡ LUNG DISEASE
- ♡ KIDNEY DISEASE
- ♡ ALLERGIES TO MEDICATIONS

- ♡ HEARING LOSS
- ♡ HIGH BLOOD PRESSURE
- ♡ PHYSICAL ABNORMALITIES
- ♡ STROKE
- ♡ VISION LOSS
- ♡ ASTHMA
- ♡ DIABETES
- ♡ HEART DISEASE
- ♡ VERY TALL OR VERY SHORT STATURE
    - *Compared to the rest of the family
- ♡ BIRTH MARKS
- ♡ BLOOD CLOTTING DISORDERS
- ♡ ALZHEIMER'S/DIMENTIA
- ♡ GOUT

www.ingramcontent.com/pod-product-compliance
Lightning Source LLC
Chambersburg PA
CBHW081725250726
48657CB00010B/3133